WAKE
THE
BRIDE

WAKE
THE
BRIDE

JEFF KINLEY

HARVEST HOUSE PUBLISHERS
EUGENE, OREGON

Cover by Harvest House Publishers Inc., Eugene, Oregon

Cover photo © Igor Zh. / Shutterstock

Published in association with William K. Jensen Literary Agency, 119 Bampton Court, Eugene, Oregon 97404.

WAKE THE BRIDE

Copyright © 2015 Jeff Kinley
Published by Harvest House Publishers
Eugene, Oregon 97408
www.harvesthousepublishers.com
Library of Congress Cataloging-in-Publication Data
    Kinley, Jeff.
    Wake the bride / Jeff Kinley.
        pages cm
    ISBN 978-0-7369-6516-3 (pbk.)
    ISBN 978-0-7369-6517-0 (eBook)
    1. Bible. Revelation—Commentaries. 2. Bible. Revelation—Criticism, interpretation, etc. I. Title.
    BS2825.53.K56 2015
    228'.06—dc23
                                                                        2015006025

Printed in the United States of America

21 22 23 24 25 26 / GP-JH / 10 9 8 7 6 5 4

To all those who wear the fine linen.
"Blessed is the one who stays awake…"

Revelation 16:15

Contents

Introduction 9

1. A Day Is Coming 13

2. The "New" Jesus 25

3. Wedding Dress 41

4. Grounding the Rapture 57

5. The Bridegroom Comes! 67

6. Gold, Silver, and Bronze 83

7. Meanwhile, in Heaven…a Throne 103

8. Rebels and Wrath 119

9. Satan's Celebrity 135

10. Return Engagement! 151

11. Heaven *Is* for Real,
    But You Haven't Been There…Yet 165

12. The Beauty Awakes 183

Notes 199

Contents

Introduction

The French poet Paul Valéry, describing the pessimism arising from post-World War I Europe, wrote, "The future, like everything else, is not what it used to be."

One hundred years later, his words have fresh meaning. The future has never been more uncertain. Never more unknown. Never more volatile. And yet, despite this ambiguity, we remain fascinated with the future, fixated on discovering what the world will be like *then*...in the "post-now." There's a natural intrigue regarding what's going to happen to this terrestrial ball we're inhabiting. But why? Why is the future (and more importantly, the subject of the end times) so interesting? Why does it captivate our attention? Why do we get that deer-in-the-headlights stare whenever some TV show, blockbuster movie, or best-selling book on the subject crosses our path?

I suspect it has something to do with our inherent human curiosity. We're wired to *know*. And the future is, by definition, *not* known. We don't like that, so we seek to satisfy that curiosity by creating lifelike fantasy scenarios giving our imagination a temporary fix. Hollywood has smartly tapped into this curiosity by creating epic, futuristic productions. Though pure conjecture, these films tap into the human psyche, temporarily fulfilling our longing to know what the future will be like. It's these imaginary scenarios of the apocalypse or postapocalypse that draw us (and our debit cards) to the box office.

But unlike fictional books or fantasy movies, Scripture's prophecies are not portrayals or predictions of things that *might* happen. Instead, they're visual previews of events Jesus Himself declared "*must* soon take place."[1] Backstage passes to coming attractions. If the Bible is true and can be understood literally, then the events foretold in Revelation are prophetic truths our generation must know and respond to.

If we are indeed rapidly approaching the end of days, could Jesus presently be preparing His bride for such a time?

Chances are you're one of those curious souls not satisfied with being left in the dark, imagining, guessing, hoping. You're hungry for some concrete confidence concerning the last days of planet Earth and the return of Jesus Christ.

This book will help satisfy that hunger. It fills that void where your voyeuristic curiosity dwells, replacing it with knowledge and truth. It won't answer every trivial detail about the end times, but what you see and learn about the future will be enough to change you *in the now*. Journeying through these pages, you'll experience a head-on collision with history...in advance. A sneak preview into the future. It's the ultimate reality drama, only this one isn't staged.

This is the real deal.

And every bit of it is going to happen.

But knowing about the end times does more than just satisfy your sweet tooth for prophecy. These truths will strengthen your faith in the accuracy of Scripture. Your confidence in the Bible will rise, giving you a firm conviction concerning the Book you love.

These end-time realities will also reveal the wise plans and purposes of God. And though His judgments are often beyond understanding and His ways deeper than our minds can fathom, there's still plenty to know and digest.[2] You'll see God's view of things to come, gaining through His eyes a clearer perspective on humanity, the church, and your own life. And you'll have a brand-new lens through which to see and interpret world news.

Prophecy tells us what's going to happen before it happens. Some people in God's long story have been privileged to see prophecy fulfilled in their lifetime, while others have had to believe by faith that certain things would one day come to pass. Others have even suffered for those beliefs, considered fools for believing in what many labeled as ridiculous fantasies.

Right, Noah?

Encountering Revelation's prophecies will guard us against lies, half-truths, crazy ideas, and end-times rumors. No doubt our adversary would try to deceive us into chasing fads and trends leading us to believe things not found in Scripture. Therefore, we must stick to the script, keeping us from falling prey to false or imagined theories about the future.

These prophecies also give us great comfort and peace in uncertain times. Knowing that God Himself is orchestrating history brings calm in the midst of a gathering global storm.

Perhaps best of all, prophecy also inspires us toward a different kind of life. Not one where we hop into our pajamas and climb the nearest mountain to wait for Jesus's return, but one that motivates us toward personal purity and preparation for the One who promised to come back for us.[3]

Make no mistake about it—Revelation was intended to be read *and* obeyed. Just as much as Psalms, Philippians, and the Gospels. Though much of it is prophetic, those prophecies nevertheless carry a message for us now. Revelation was written *to* the church and *for* the church. And if you're a believer in Jesus, that means you.

As you read, expect to develop not only a deep concern for your world and friends, but also a fresh excitement for your life. Like those original, first-century Christians, you'll begin living with a sense of urgency and expectancy, infused with a massive dose of hope. And like the aged apostle John, you may find yourself exclaiming, "Amen. Come, Lord Jesus."[4]

But for Jesus's bride to experience this, she must first wake up.

1

A Day Is Coming

One day. And the world is never the same.
D-day
November 22, 1963
9/11

Days like these imprint generations, shaping the destinies of nations. They impact global culture, and like those still-visible D-day bomb craters along the Normandy coast, they transform the landscape, becoming lasting reminders to the colossal difference a day can make.

But according to our Bible, there are more significant days than D-day ahead for us. Dates and times on heaven's calendar that are indelibly preset. Moments to come in which everything—and I mean *everything*—will change.

We occasionally mention these times in the church. Prophetic events do have a place in our Christian experience. But biblical prophecies can often seem seasonal, stored in the same church closet where we keep the Christmas manger and that big cross we use for the Easter presentation. Much like those holidays, Scripture's future stuff can become almost novel and, at times, even trite. We reflect on the birth, death, and resurrection of Jesus with great meaning and contemplative focus, and rightly so. These events impact us, not just because of their historical certainty, but also because these past events were meant to influence our lives in the here and now.

What often becomes difficult, however, is applying that same importance to events that have yet to take place. Because we can't schedule Scripture's predictions like we do Christmas and Easter, the average believer struggles to embrace them. We talk about "signs of the times" and use words like *rapture, tribulation,* and *last days,* but all too easily relegate them to that mental file marked "Complicated," "Too Much Mystery," or "Above My Spiritual Pay Grade." And though we may profess belief in their certain and eventual fulfillment, we fail to understand their relevance to our lives today because they seem so foggy and far off.

However, this is precisely where we can miss God's plan and purpose for prophecy. Prophecy's future realities are meant to impact us in the now. It's always been this way. Messianic prophecies given centuries before the birth of Christ gave hope, helping believers prepare and live in light of that coming reality.[1] Ignoring or treating lightly God's future events lulls us into a spirit of complacency, slumber, and unpreparedness. But God wants His people to be awake...and prepared.

Ezekiel was appointed as a spiritual watchman who upon seeing approaching danger was to blow the trumpet, alerting Israel.[2] Jesus urged His followers to adopt the same attitude. In describing the events of the end times to His disciples in Mark 13, the Lord repeatedly urges them to "see" (v. 5), "be on your guard" (v. 9), "be on guard" (v. 23), "be on guard, keep awake" (v. 33), "stay awake" (v. 35), "lest [the master of the house] come suddenly and find you asleep" (v. 36). He concludes, "And what I say to you I say to all: Stay awake."[3]

Just days later, Christ would lead them to the Garden of Gethsemane where, after returning from a time of prayer, He found them fast asleep. Jesus's response in this important moment of His life was anything but cordial.

> "Simon, are you *asleep*? Could you not *keep watch* for one hour? *Keep watching* and praying that you may not come into temptation; the spirit is willing, but the flesh is weak." Again He went away and prayed, saying the same words. And again He came and found them *sleeping*, for their eyes were very heavy; and they did not know what to answer Him. And He came the third time, and said to them, "Are you *still sleeping* and *resting*? It is enough; the hour has come; behold, the Son of Man is being betrayed into the hands of sinners. *Get up*, let us be going; behold, the one who betrays Me is at hand!"[4]

The disciples' hearts may have been sincere, but they lacked the stamina to stay awake. Their eyes were heavy. They were sluggish. Lethargic. Lacking vigilance. Furthermore, they didn't "get it" either, failing to grasp the historic weight of the moment. They had no clue how earthshaking the following day would be. Even after some three years with Jesus, they still couldn't comprehend how critical that near-future event would be to them...and to all humankind.

It makes you wonder how closely they had been listening to Jesus all along.

Are we listening?

Just the previous day, during the final week of His life, Jesus had gathered His disciples together on a Jerusalem hillside called the Mount of Olives. There they asked Him about His coming kingdom, and specifically about the signs leading up to the end of the age. Part of the Lord's answer involved a fascinating story about ten virgin bridesmaids.[5]

The Jewish custom of the day was for the bridegroom to surprise the bride by snatching her away from her house and leading her in a procession to the wedding festivities and their new home. Attending the bride were young, unmarried maidens. In this story, Jesus says these ten bridesmaids were equipped with lamps in the event of a surprise night wedding procession. Five of these young women had purchased oil for their lamps and five had not. When the bridegroom seemed to delay his arrival, all ten girls became drowsy and fell asleep. Then suddenly, at midnight there was a shout.

"Behold the bridegroom! Come out to meet him."

But while running out to fulfill their duty and light their lamps, five of the bridesmaids realized they had forgotten to purchase oil. After trying to persuade the others to share some of theirs and being denied, they headed into the night searching for oil. In the meantime, the bridegroom led the prepared virgins away to the wedding feast. When the unprepared bridesmaids finally arrived outside the celebration, they found the door shut. They pleaded, "Lord, lord, open up for us." But the groom replied without hesitation, "Truly I say to you, I do not know you."[6] Jesus then turns to His disciples with a sobering warning, "Be on the alert then, for you do not know the day nor the hour."

Are we prepared?

Dr. Luke recounts the story of a young man who, while Paul spoke at a church gathering, fell asleep and tumbled out of a third-story window to his death. This kid didn't have narcolepsy. He just gradually dozed off. Young Eutychus was lulled to sleep even while surrounded by the truth.[7]

Are we awake?

Paul repeatedly urged New Testament believers to fight spiritual drowsiness, especially as it relates to spiritual warfare, the end times, and the return of Christ.

- "With all prayer and petition pray at all times in the Spirit…*be on the alert* with all perseverance."[8]

- "So then *let us not sleep* as others do, but let us *be alert* and sober."[9]

Peter warned Christians scattered across Asia Minor,

- "Therefore, prepare your minds for action, *keep sober in spirit*, fix your hope completely on the grace to be brought to you at the *revelation of Jesus Christ.*"[10]
- "The *end of all things is near*; therefore, be of sound judgment and *sober spirit* for the purpose of prayer."[11]

Are we alert?

So Jesus places a high value on His bride being watchful, ready, and awake. But why? The answer is found in Revelation. In fact, that's exactly why this last book of the Bible was written—to provide believers like you and me with a verbal panorama of the end times, and to motivate the church to prepare herself for the imminent return of her bridegroom. Part of the New Testament's majestic symphony of theology, Revelation plays a huge part in describing the pivotal, prophetic days that lay ahead for planet Earth.

I believe the next prophetic event will occur when our Lord returns like a bridegroom, snatching up His bride and taking her to heaven prior to global judgments being unleashed upon our world.[12] According to Scripture, this dramatic day will set in motion a series of catastrophic happenings outlined in Revelation 4–18. And all this is merely the opening act leading up to the main event, the climactic moment of history itself.

The Second Coming of Jesus Christ

Though many scenes described in Revelation are not yet fully understood, grasping every detail is not necessary in order to get the big picture. And knowing how all these prophecies will play out isn't needed in order to know how we should live. In fact, even though I don't believe the church will endure the judgments unfolding during the seven-year period known as the tribulation, those judgments nonetheless impact us today. But more about that later.

So here's the big idea. You may think Revelation is off limits for you, reserved only for PhDs and PNTs (Prophecy Nerd-Types). Perhaps you've experienced sensory overload from Bible teachers armed with confusing charts and drawings of ten-headed beasts. Or maybe you've been turned off by wild-eyed TV preachers predicting the identity of the Antichrist or describing giant "grasshopper demons" in Revelation 9. Or you may have no idea what Scripture says concerning the future of the church or planet Earth.

Whatever the case, don't despair. God originally wrote Revelation to Christians living at the end of the first century. These believers lived in a day when both their government and culture were hostile to those professing faith in Jesus. So He gave them this—His final book. It was intended to be read aloud, and like all Scripture, designed to teach, reprove, correct, and train us in righteousness.[13]

And though much of it is prophetic and sometimes puzzling, even what is presently unclear serves an important role in believers' lives, both then and now. Throughout the mind-blowing, apocalyptic vision found in Revelation, a natural spirit of expectancy rises in the hearts of those who engage it. Jesus's Revelation produces in us a deep longing for His return, and a heart that cries out for Him to "come."[14] Those first-century disciples *expected* their Lord to return at any moment, and were daily "looking for that blessed hope and the appearing of the glory of our great God and Savior, Christ Jesus."[15] *Are we looking?*

My friend, Jesus Christ is returning to retrieve and rescue His bride! God's judgment on our world cannot be avoided, and His Son's return cannot be delayed. This announcement ought to invigorate our minds and hearts. It should raise our spiritual heartbeat in anticipation and stimulate our soul to alert status. Yes, there really is another climactic Day coming, one making all previous red-letter dates pale in comparison. And it may appear on history's horizon much sooner than we realize.

So if God wants us to be *awake*, exactly how do we open our eyes? How does a believer learn to see?

The Perils of Prophecy

Not long ago, I was in El Paso visiting my son, an army officer stationed at Ft. Bliss. While there, our family decided to hike up the Franklin Mountains. I was curious about an historic site located on one of the mountain's upper slopes. Some sixty years ago, a Convair B-36 Peacemaker bomber crashed there on a frigid December afternoon a few weeks before Christmas 1953, killing all nine crewmembers.[16]

The Air Force dispatched a team to the site, eventually recovering what was left of the servicemen's bodies. They also retrieved a portion of the tail section, along with classified bits and pieces of the bomber. The remaining wreckage was left as it was at fifty-two hundred feet, scattered wildly across the side of the mountain range. A mute monument to a tragic military aviation disaster.

Now I found myself about to ascend the mountain and try to locate the historic crash site. Even though the hike was described as "very strenuous," I casually brushed it off as a pretty easy climb. I purchased a cheap hat at a local outdoor market, laced up my hiking shoes, and grabbed a bottle of water to quench my thirst in the sweltering summer heat.

We discovered the first part of the hike involved a half-mile walk up a trail snaking its way along the base of the mountain. A gradual incline, this rocky footpath proved to be much longer and more difficult than I had anticipated. Having previously researched it, I had already predetermined our eventual destination...*generally speaking.* Even so, there was no actual trail leading up to the site. But no big deal, right? Well, maybe, unless you realize this is no ordinary hike.

The Franklin Mountains are in the desert, a precarious terrain liberally littered with prickly pear cacti and a plentiful supply of Spanish daggers, a plant with long, swordlike leaves. Encounter one of these hard needle tips, and you don't forget it.

Loose rocks made an already unsteady, nonexistent path even more perilous. So steep is the mountain grade that one misstep, and I would be rapidly tumbling head over feet, collecting thorns and accumulating broken bones along the way.

Oh, and did I mention there are rattlesnakes? I hate snakes. *Hate* them. Every rock overhang I passed gave me caution, fearing the sudden strike of poisonous fangs at my ankles.

Like some ancient mythological goddess, the mountain stands stoic and stern. She is treacherous and unforgiving and cares not for the occasional hiker. She dares you to ascend her and welcomes all challengers with a silent sneer that seems to whisper, "Bring it."

Needless to say, I chose my steps with great precision and caution. And because of the altitude, I was also forced to take frequent stops to catch my breath. More than once, I wondered to myself if this excursion was worth the effort. Would I make it? Was I crazy for even attempting such a hike? Was I going to regret this?

"One step at a time," I kept repeating.

And so, stopping for a moment to extract some oxygen from the thin mountain air, I collapsed on a large rock and took a well-deserved drink from my water bottle. Dropping my head, I stared at the scorching sand beneath my shoes.

And that's when I saw it.

Gleaming in the afternoon sun was a small object protruding between the rocks and sand. I bent down, digging and probing with my walking stick. What I eventually unearthed proved to be a small spring, about a half-inch in length, broken and encrusted with rust.

Though I didn't know exactly how long it had been buried there, of one thing I was certain—it had come literally *from the sky*. Something really big had birthed this metal fragment. Something that disintegrated into a million pieces sixty years earlier.

This insignificant fragment proved to be a tiny clue, and one pointing to a much greater reality. It was confirmation that if I just kept moving forward and upward, I would eventually find what I was searching for. Six decades ago, the world's largest bomber crashed into the Franklin Mountains. And now I was holding a piece of it in my hand.

After another forty-five minutes, I finally reached the crash site and discovered what past hikers and explorers had found—huge landing gear, a giant, twisted propeller, a crushed jet turbine, and mangled pieces of melted fuselage and metal—all randomly scattered across the mountainside. These silent sentries hold perpetual vigil over the spot where nine servicemen stepped into eternity all those years ago.

But not everyone who traverses this terrain makes it to the crash site. Some have no idea where they're going or what they're actually looking for. They are content to remain on the marked trail along the mountain's base, unaware what lies some thirteen hundred feet above them.

Others who make the climb unknowingly step right over important clues along the way. They misread the mountain and end up in a different place altogether. Some begin the climb, only to discover it's much more challenging than it looks and turn back too soon, forfeiting the amazing discovery and vantage point awaiting them at journey's end.

But for those determined souls who carry on—persevering and pushing through the heat, altitude, rugged terrain, fatigue, and threat of injury—those who carefully observe the signs and clues along the way—those who navigate the treacherous journey,

22   WAKE THE BRIDE

believing it leads to a worthwhile destination—*these* seekers are rewarded with an encounter like none other. And here's why: the higher and farther you go in this uphill expedition, the more you know. The clues start out small, but they get bigger the closer you get to the point of impact. Journeying upward, the crash's debris increase in size and frequency, indicating you're getting close to your destination. And your heart races in anticipation.

But the thing is, you never really know what the next step will bring.

Prophecy Peak

I find that Revelation and Bible prophecy are very much like the Franklin Mountains. They seem foreboding. Intimidating. In the clouds. Unapproachable. Unconquerable. The kind of thing only experts ascend while the rest of us gaze at it in wonder from a safe distance. We stare at such mountains in wild-eyed amazement, often settling for a well-framed selfie or a postcard at the gift shop down below.

Even so, like a huge mountain, prophecy remains, and it's not going away. From its peaks it calls to you, producing a natural yet strange curiosity. It beckons you to explore. To understand. And yet you hesitate, unsure of your hiking skills. You think if you try, you might not make it to the top and comprehend God's prophetic plan.

But others have been there and know the way. You won't walk alone on this journey. Together, we'll make the climb, and Scripture will be our personal guide, pointing out the dangerous places as we progress.

Much like hikers, those attempting to scale "Revelation Mountain" typically fall into several categories. Some believe in last days' prophecy, but choose to keep their distance, safely remaining in the valley below. They've concluded that Revelation and prophecy are far too complex for anyone to really understand. So they settle for general truth—"Jesus is coming back...I hope. And that's enough for me!" So they remain in virtual ignorance about things to come. But this does very little for their present lives or future confidence.

Other truth-seekers begin their prophecy journey well, but get lost along the way. This often happens because they are not properly equipped for the trip. Their lack of biblical understanding hinders their advance up the mountain. They don't know the difference between a discarded candy-bar wrapper and a clue. They're unable to effectively read the terrain, and thus fail to navigate it accurately.

There are hikers who come to the trailhead well-equipped, but with the wrong mindset. Preconceived ideas, personal preferences, and faulty interpretations eventually lead them to false conclusions. These are the guys who claim to have identified the antichrist or who place leaflets under your windshield wipers announcing the exact date for Jesus's return. They seem to know a lot more than the Bible does. Guides like these will get you lost in a hurry.

Yes, Revelation can be a foreboding mountain, especially when you live life in the valley below. But you *can* understand it. This book will be somewhat of a hike, one that involves exploring the clues God has scattered throughout Scripture and history—evidence and signs pointing to the truth about the end times and the return of His Son, Jesus. And though it may at times seem random, everything has a place and a purpose. Together, we'll pause to consider the pieces He has left for us, both large and small.

But I will give you a heads up. This journey is not without its perils. There will be obstacles and unknowns along the way. Not every path is clearly marked. At times you will wonder how a particular piece fits into the end-times puzzle. And as we journey along, you will feel the gravity of the path you're on. And the air does get thin up there. Thorny truths of divine judgment and the end of life as we know it will prick your mind and conscience. What you discover may sting a bit, even disturb your spirit. You might even grow short of breath. But that's natural, and okay. It's during those times you'll need to pause, put the book down, and contemplate the magnitude of what you're discovering. It's perhaps during those breathers when you'll make even more discoveries—about God, the future, and especially your own life.

But no worries. We won't get stranded. If you continue up the mountain with me, I promise your perseverance will be rewarded. So if you're ready, then gear up, lace up, and hydrate.

And let's go.

2

The "New" Jesus

t's been calculated that 28 percent of Scripture was prophecy at the time it was written. That's over a fourth of the Bible. With over 1800 prophecies in Scripture taking up over 8300 verses, including 1239 prophecies in the Old Testament and 578 in the New Testament, that's a lot of verses! Only four of the sixty-six books of the Bible are without prophecy—Ruth, the Song of Solomon, Philemon, and 3 John. Even the shortest book of the Bible mentions prophecy.[1] From the first book (Genesis) to the last (Revelation), Scripture's pages are literally filled with truth about the future. God even chose to complete His Word to humanity with an entire book devoted to prophecy.

Footprints of the Future

Though much of biblical prophecy has already been fulfilled, Revelation's prophetic chapters speak of things that haven't happened yet. Apparently, revealing truth about future events is something God likes to do. He actually wants His people to know what's going to happen in the days ahead and what's in store for us and our world. But why? What's His rationale behind this?

One reason God gives us prophecy is so we can have *hope* in the midst of uncertain times.[2] Prophecy also gives us *faith* and *assurance* in God Himself. Knowing the Lord is in charge of writing and directing history enables us to continue moving forward in life. His sovereign control frees us from panicking or worrying about the future. And that's always a good thing. Sometimes God's prophets foretold events that would happen in the near future, while at other times their divine predictions revealed events that would take place hundreds, even thousands of years later. But either way, God would steer the course of history.

Another thing prophecy does is instill us with *confidence* in God's Word. The Bible has an amazing 100 percent accuracy record with prophecy. Every single past prophecy has come true—*literally* and *exactly* as the Bible predicted it would. So if that's true, why shouldn't we expect those "not yet fulfilled" prophecies to do the same? This fact enables us to bank on the accuracy of God's Word.

Still another reason why He gives us prophecy is so we can *prepare* ourselves. God's word to Noah motivated the father of three to spend the next 120 years preparing a boat so he and his family could survive God's future flood judgment. What you'll learn in the pages that follow will help prepare you as well—not only for God's next prophetic event, but also for how to live until that time. And with this knowledge comes not dread or despair but a sense of anticipation and excitement.

That's why Revelation was written. John wrote down what he saw and heard in this apocalyptic vision from Jesus. And why did Jesus do this? Because His church was fast asleep as her wedding day approached. The bridegroom wanted His bride awake, alert, pure, and fervently in love with Him at the end of the age. But by AD 90, only a few short generations after her birth, the church had grown cold, self-absorbed...and *asleep*.

The truths of Revelation—*all* of them—are meant to wake the church so she can prepare herself to meet the groom. And so Jesus delivers this last book of the Bible as a quad-shot of espresso to a slumbering bride. To jolt her awake because Someone is coming quickly, and His reward is with Him.[3]

But exactly who is this Revelation bridegroom? And what is He like? We're about to find out.

And so as we begin our truth-climb up the mountain, God will outfit you in His truth like a good pair of hiking shoes, giving you traction as you travel. He will infuse you with encouragement as you go forward, giving you assurance in your direction and confidence in your course. Fully prepared, you'll grow in your excitement for what awaits you at journey's end.

Hype and His Story

Unbelievable and even bizarre claims are often made about the events recorded in the Bible's last book. There's no shortage of carnival barkers in the circus that often surrounds the end times and Jesus's Second Coming. There's also plenty of legend and speculation surrounding Christ's *first* arrival in our world, including some outright myths and fables. For example, those wise men (the Bible never says there were three of them), rather than presenting their gifts to a baby in a manger, didn't find Jesus until He was around two years old.[4] Other common assumptions include: Mary riding on a donkey, Jesus being born on December 25, and angels singing. Actually, none of these are mentioned in Scripture; rather, they have become a part of happy tradition and folklore.

Today, we've effectively commercialized Messiah's birth, marketing it as a religious, romanticized, sentimental tale of stars, shepherds, drummer boys, and a silent baby surrounded by spice kings and smiling animals.

Hype.

Don't misunderstand. It's certainly appropriate to celebrate Jesus's incarnation. But many church members forget that this baby Jesus grew up. He navigated His way through the awkwardness of adolescence, eventually becoming an adult, spending the last three years of His life teaching, revealing God, performing miracles, and loving the unlovely. He was arrested, tried, tortured, and butchered before being spike-nailed to a rough-hewn wooden crossbeam. Then, according to the Bible, He rose from the dead. That is the Jesus most Christians are also very familiar with. We can close our eyes and easily envision a manger, a beard, a miracle, a cross, and an empty tomb. No problem, right?

But I'd like to introduce you to a completely different image of Jesus than we're used to seeing. This Christ you may not be quite as familiar with. He isn't crying in a manger, teaching on a hillside, healing blind men, or suffering on a cross. We know about this particular Jesus from an experience the apostle John had, carefully recorded for us in the book of Revelation.[5]

What we're about to hear may sound like the rants of a crazy old man, or the writings of some ancient cult leader, religious propagandist, or creative scriptwriter working on the next Hollywood blockbuster. But none of these would be accurate. Instead, what you're about to discover comes straight from the Bible that sits on your desk or bedside table. This subject matter will likely arouse your curiosity, challenge your thinking, and possibly even disturb your spirit. But if you dare, digest Scripture's words and ask yourself the question, "Could all this really be true?"

No hype this time. Just some holy history.

The apostle John was advanced in years, well into his midnineties. This is the same John who wrote the Gospel of John and 1, 2, and 3 John. We catch up with him on an island in the Aegean Sea called Patmos. He's been banished there because of his faith in Jesus Christ and his preaching.[6] While there, God gives John a bizarre, apocalyptic vision. A vision is like a very vivid, HD dream, only you're awake. So John takes pen in hand and writes down what he sees and hears in this vision, delivered to him by an angel messenger.[7] In doing so, he describes Jesus in various ways and with many names, such as "eternal," "faithful witness," "ruler of the kings of the earth," and the "one who loves us." Jesus refers to Himself in this vision as the "Alpha and the Omega...who is and who was and who is to come, the Almighty."[8] *Alpha* and *omega* are the first and last letters of the Greek alphabet, signifying Jesus Christ as the beginning and end—in whom dwells the sum total of all truth. His mind is infinite and His understanding cannot be measured. He knows everything that was, is, and is to come. He also knows all possibilities, contingencies, and what-ifs. Theologians call this *omniscience*. I call it mind-blowing, the mere contemplation of which overwhelms me.

John's description of this Jesus is pretty intimidating as it tells us He is the eternal God. The implications of such a claim are beyond profound, and if true, effectively exclude and disqualify every other religious founder, philosopher, and belief system in history. He alone possesses ultimate credibility. Scripture, and Jesus Himself, repeatedly assert this claim that He alone is God.[9]

In fact, everything we'll discover together in Revelation rests on this foundational truth. The essence, identity, and character of Jesus Christ comprise the cornerstone upon which all end-times prophecy is built. If He truly is God, then His Word is true and trustworthy, and all of Revelation is believable and destined to become reality. Consequently, then, Christ alone possesses the wisdom and power to bring all these future things to pass.

However, if Jesus is not who He claimed to be, then nothing in Revelation can be trusted. In which case, not much else about Him really matters, and John is, at best, a senile old man with a vivid imagination. He's just seeing things.

Fortunately, Jesus validated His identity and claims to deity by rising from the dead. All that is needed to collapse Christianity for good is to adequately explain away the resurrection.

Good luck with that.

20/20 Vision

The entire book of Revelation is a vision given *by* Jesus Christ *to* John *through* an angel *for* the church.[10] Most of Revelation's chapters are prophetic, or simply "history written in advance." In this book, John was told to write what he saw, and to deliver the message to seven specific churches located in Asia Minor. He begins by reminding us of one more bold claim in Jesus's repertoire—a promise to return to this world someday. [11]

That's *your* world, by the way. Christ says His return will be globally visible and that "every eye will see Him." That statement sounded unbelievable twenty years ago. Your parents' and grandparents' generations never could have imagined how something like this could ever be possible. But with rapid advances in technology and communication, including your smartphone, it is now entirely believable.[12]

Even so, a lot of what we'll see together in Revelation will sound unbelievable. Maybe even too sci-fi to be real. But Jesus stakes His very character on the certainty of every word of it being true.[13] That's yet another bold claim, especially considering all that Revelation will show us concerning the last days and beyond.

John's revelation continues, becoming more intense. He sees Jesus the Christ as He is right now—in heaven, glorified and exalted. Those words may sound religious, but don't gloss over them. They simply mean this: Everything that has ever existed—heaven, earth, nature, man, beast, and the entire universe—points to Jesus the Christ. They give Him all the credit and applause. Paul echoes this, writing that Christ is the reason for everything that exists.[14] All things have been created by Him and for Him.[15] He is the point of every living thing, and the very reason for our existence.

Scripture adds that His mysterious power even holds the universe together, both at the micro and macro level.[16] How awesome must this Jesus be if everything owes its existence and purpose to

Him. Do you feel the weight of this truth? It seems that already the air is getting thinner on our climb, and we've just begun!

John now gets even more specific in his description of this heavenly, exalted Jesus. He sees a flowing robe, reaching down to His feet.[17] This speaks of Jesus's role as high priest and judge of all mankind.[18] The Galilean carpenter is done with passing out free fish and bread to the masses and healing crippled beggars. Now He's in heaven, preparing Himself to judge the earth and all its inhabitants.

In this vision of John's, Jesus's head and hair are white like wool.[19] Can you picture that? Does that seem strange? In Proverbs, Solomon wrote, "A gray head is a crown of glory; it is found in the way of righteousness."[20] This image of Jesus illustrates His unimaginable depth of wisdom and the respect due Him. He alone possesses the wisdom of the ages.[21] He is the supernatural sage, the original and primary source of all wise thought.

Next, John peers into the eyes of this glorified Christ and sees a flame of fire. This penetrating gaze sees beyond the surface, past our words and deeds, right into our souls. There, He reads not only our thoughts but also our motives.[22] His eyes CAT scan our spirits, x-raying our hearts. Literally *nothing* is hidden from his sight.[23] It is these very eyes of fiery judgment that millions of His enemies will encounter when He bursts through the clouds at His Second Coming.[24] That thought alone causes me to shudder in respect and holy reverence. More about this terrifying and awesome event later.

John now describes Christ's feet, which are like "burnished bronze" or "fine brass" (nkjv).[25] In the Old Testament tabernacle, there was an altar covered with brass, and when heated up, would become glowing hot.[26] Again, this illustrates His strong stand in divine judgment. It's a judgment that has been held back for centuries by His persevering patience and love.[27]

Previously, John heard the voice of Jesus like a loud trumpet.[28] In the ancient world, whenever a king would arrive, a loud trumpet would sound. This meant royalty was officially "in the house." But now that Jesus has John's full attention, the Lord's voice changes. Having already announced His arrival and presence, His voice now more closely resembles mighty ocean waves crashing into a rocky shore.[29]

A few years ago, I took my son Stuart on a trip to California to celebrate his college graduation. While there, we drove down California's famous Highway 1, stopping at scenic spots along the way. The views we witnessed together were absolutely breathtaking. One such location is Point Lobos, located in Carmel. We pulled over and hiked a bit before climbing out on the huge rocks. We stood there, watching in silence as mighty Pacific Ocean waves slammed into the jagged California coastline. Over and over again, their incessant crashing sang a song of majesty, announcing each wave's faithful arrival on the rocky shore. You simply can't witness this scene without experiencing a deep sense of awe and wonder at the power and authority of the ocean. And you realize all the more how small and weak you are.

Roaring waves are a picture of never-ending strength. Since John was exiled to an island in the Mediterranean Sea, he was also likely familiar with that sound. This voice in John's ears was a constant reminder of the presence and power of the Almighty, similar to what Ezekiel experienced in his own mind-blowing vision from God.[30] And with every wave of Jesus's authoritative words, John experienced deep awe and wonder.

It's this same power and authority that sets up the next image in John's vision. He sees Jesus holding "seven stars in His right hand."[31] We learn a little later that these stars represent the pastors of seven churches Jesus is about to address. These were actual churches in Asia Minor at the time. These pastors were given such a designation because they were commissioned with the task of shining God's character and glory here on earth through their pastoral ministries. We'll learn more about these churches in the next chapter.

[handwritten margin note: Ezekiel 43:2]

John's attention is now diverted back toward Jesus's authoritative voice. With wild-eyed wonder, he sees something coming out of the Lord's mouth. It's a sharp, double-edged sword, reminding us of Hebrews 4:12, "For the word of God is alive and active. Sharper than any double-edged sword, it penetrates even to dividing soul and spirit, joints and marrow; it judges the thoughts and attitudes of the heart."

God always speaks truth. And His truth-sword cuts and penetrates no matter which way it's swinging. There are no dull edges on this double-edged blade. Sometimes His words comfort and bring healing. But other times they hurt, convicting us, even wounding and waging war against us. They cut through the surface, past the shallow places of our minds and hearts, piercing into the deepest part of who we are. His words diagnose the diseases within us.

Here in Revelation 1, this symbolic sword pictures the unbreakable clarity, accuracy, depth, and power of Jesus's words. Swords aren't made for display or show, but rather for battle. They are intended to cut and penetrate.[32] Here, His words are about to reveal the state of His bride, the church. Jesus's evaluation of the church, then and now, will likely strike a familiar chord with you.

Finally, John describes Jesus's face as "the sun shining in all its brilliance."[33] It is virtually impossible for us to imagine the glory of this God, or remotely conceive in our tiny brains what it must be like. "Glory" is such a nebulous concept, hard to put into words. But as with our own sun, John is unable to look directly at Jesus's blinding brilliance for very long. His radiance and glow are beyond the stars and the sun itself (pause here to let your brain cool down from considering that truth). However, the glory of this Christ is more than just a visual experience alone. I believe John actually *feels* this glory. Like the penetrating warmth of the sun, John experiences the emanation of God's glorious brilliance deep in his spirit. And this is intentional. God is not an object to be viewed but a Person to be experienced. Though we walk by faith, God created and designed all our senses with purpose. He did this so we could experience Him and the gifts He's created for us to enjoy. Touch, sight, sound, smell, and taste are all given to us so we can experience God and the things in life He gives to us.[34] We'll encounter all these senses as we hike through Revelation.

God's glory isn't just something to look at or admire from a distance like some painted masterpiece hanging in a museum. Nonsense! He wants every part of us to experience who He is, to be impacted by His glory, enjoying Him in the process.[35] And those who know Him can find this ultimate delight in that relationship. All these great gifts we experience from a God who is *glorious*.

However, in this unique vision, John is traumatized after being exposed to Christ's glory. Instead of delight, the cumulative effect of seeing this fresh image of Jesus devastates the beloved disciple. And like others previously exposed to God's glory, John falls at Jesus's feet like a dead man.[36] The sheer intensity of seeing this Jesus was more than he could handle, causing his body and consciousness to go into sensory overload and temporarily shut down. Jesus understands John's condition and comforts him, telling him not to be afraid.[37]

I believe this is one reason why God will have to give us brand-new, supernatural bodies upon entering heaven.[38] Without them we could never withstand the intensity of being exposed to His spectacular glory. What a thought!

Scripture's description of seeing the glorified and exalted Christ is radically different from modern-day supposed visits to heaven. Meeting this Jesus is not a casual, flippant encounter, but a catastrophic shock to the spirit and senses. Here, John is allowed to write about what he saw, whereas Paul and others in the Bible were prevented from sharing a word about their heavenly visit.

In short, John was blown away.

If this is how a longtime devoted follower and friend reacted, can you imagine what an unbeliever will experience when at death they come face-to-face with the glorified Son of God? OK, that's heavy. But the point is that, unlike during His time on earth, people are not immediately drawn to this Jesus we encounter in Revelation. Not even believers, including apostles, initially approach this Jesus. This causes me to believe our first reaction upon seeing the glorified Christ in heaven will be to fall on our faces in profound wonder and worship.

But even though Jesus places a comforting hand on John, telling him not to be afraid, He nevertheless continues with His revelation, even turning up the intimidation factor, confidently announcing, "I am the First and the Last. I am the Living One; I was dead, and now look, I am alive for ever and ever! And I hold the keys of death and Hades."[39]

Despite the fact that John had already seen Christ following His resurrection,[40] Jesus nevertheless proclaims Himself as alive from the dead. I believe He did this for three reasons:

First, he knows how susceptible we are to doubt and skepticism, even about things we've experienced firsthand or believe to be true. We're human, and thus naturally weak and forgetful.

Second, the truth of the resurrection never gets old. It's not just an Easter thing, but an everyday thing. It's the ultimate good news for mankind and anyone who wonders about the afterlife. Let's be clear. If Jesus's corpse was still in the grave around AD 95 (when John wrote this), then nothing about Christianity makes sense. As Paul so eloquently put it, if Jesus isn't alive, "your faith is futile; you are still in your sins. Then those also who have fallen asleep in Christ are lost. If only for this life we have hoped in Christ, we are of all people most to be pitied."[41]

Chew on that for a minute.

If Jesus's life ended tragically on a hill outside Jerusalem in AD 30, then those who believe in Him have no hope of knowing the truth about life, salvation, and heaven. None. They would still be lost and unforgiven (assuming there is a God, of course). And worst of all, they are to be pitied as idiots for putting their eternal hopes in such a fairy tale. And understandably so!

Everything about Christ and Christians stands or falls with the resurrection. It is the hinge upon which Christianity swings. Remove the resurrection and all you have is a good moral teacher who got Himself arrested and killed because He ticked off the wrong people. And while it's a nice thought for someone to say they follow His teachings, in reality He's no different than Gandhi, Buddha, Confucius or Mohammed—just another religious guru who gathered some followers, then died...like everybody else.

Without the resurrection, Jesus really isn't that special. In fact, without it, He isn't even a good man, because He told others to trust Him for salvation and their eternal destiny![42] He would actually be pretty evil to say such a thing. A lying deceiver. An imposter. A cheat. Someone who deserved to be hated, not loved. His legacy would be despised. His memory deservedly shunned, not elevated and imitated.

Without a living Jesus, *all* His words are now hollow, devoid of meaning and significance. Every teaching would be a cleverly devised scam, His deeds and motivation suspect. His mission a complete fraud.

Unless He was unaware that He was lying. If Jesus really *didn't know* He was lying about God, heaven and hell, salvation, and who He was, then He deserved to be committed to a psychiatric ward. He would be insane. And what would that make His millions of followers throughout history?

Not a pleasant thought.

These are the options. Jesus either rose from the dead or He didn't. And if He didn't, you can't call Him a good man. You shouldn't follow Him and you certainly shouldn't worship Him. He either has to be evil incarnate and a son of hell itself, or a poor, troubled Galilean with severe mental issues. There are no other alternatives, though you're welcome to try and think of some.

The only other explanation is that He *did* rise from the grave, exactly as Scripture claims and hundreds of His disciples witnessed.[43] And as He Himself reaffirmed in Revelation 1. I realize that may sound redundant, for how can anyone other than a living person claim to be alive? But He does, for the reasons I've already mentioned, and for one more.

Third, Jesus reminded John of His resurrection because He wanted John to realize that *his* life had meaning. John repeatedly uses the word *know* in his writings. Being sure of what he believed was important to him. And by this time, John had followed Jesus for over sixty years. He had endured shame and scorn, hardship and severe persecution. The ancient author and apologist Tertullian records that John was even thrown into a cauldron of boiling oil for his faith.[44] Legend says he continued preaching from the oil! And how was this former fisherman able to do all this? Because of one reason—his confident belief in a resurrected Christ.

I've often heard Christians try to prove the validity of the resurrection by stating, "People don't die for a lie." And because the disciples died martyrs' deaths, the resurrection must therefore be historically valid. But that's not necessarily true. Many people throughout history have died for lies. Followers of regimes, armies, cults, and evil religions have all been killed or killed themselves for values and ideologies they sincerely believed were true, but in reality proved to be lies or morally reprehensible philosophies.

When Islamic extremists flew planes into the Twin Towers on 9/11, they were fully convinced they were killing God's enemies and would be rewarded with seventy-two virgins in heaven. Of course, if they were wrong (and Scripture is right), they were merely evil, cold-blooded terrorist-murderers who went straight from one set of flames to another. They woke up in eternity to discover that God Almighty, the Judge of the Universe, was *Israel's* God—the ultimate phobia of every Muslim fanatic.

So Christian or not, simply believing in something enough to die for it proves only one thing—that you are a person of intense faith. Nothing more.[45] It doesn't (of necessity) validate what you believe any more than someone who sincerely believes in aliens, Santa Claus, or Scientology. That's because it's not your *faith* that makes something real, valid, or credible, but rather the *object* of your faith. If what you believe in is valid, then so is your belief.

And this is precisely what Jesus is affirming to John. He is assuring the beloved disciple that his long life of devoted service to God has not been for nothing. John's sufferings were not in vain because the One for whom he suffered conquered the grave and was standing in front of him! The object of his faith (Jesus) is alive, and therefore John's faith and loyal service are fully validated. "I am alive forevermore," Christ proclaims. That was very good news for John...and for us.

"What's more," Jesus says in Revelation 1:18, "I have the keys of death and Hades." In other words, "My resurrection means I am exactly who I claimed to be—God in human flesh. I am Yahweh of the Old Testament. King of the Universe. The undisputed Lord who overrules all other kings, lords, and those in authority."[46]

This means Jesus is in charge, not only of planet Earth, history, and humankind, but also of death itself. These "keys" Christ holds mean He possesses authority over life and death.[47] Scripture says that God has appointed a specific number of days for each person to live.[48] I certainly don't understand all the whys and hows of that. But His plan for each individual comes from an infinite wisdom. This and other mysteries belong only to Him.[49] And we, being finite, are limited in our understanding of even finite things (and *infinitely* so when compared to His unlimited understanding). We humans know very little but act as though we know a lot. How sad that puny creatures like us would pretend to know more than God Himself. That's the kind of pride He rejects.[50]

All this truth Jesus has shared about Himself thus far is but a prelude of what's coming. In reality, He's ramping up to reveal some stuff that will blow John's pre-technology mind completely away.

Jesus is getting ready to lift the veil off prophecies and secrets kept hidden for thousands of years. This includes revelations about the present and mysteries concerning the future. Christ will give John insight into "the things which are" and terrifying revelations about "the things which will take place after these things."

Jesus essentially says, "John, pick up your pen and write this down for the generations that will come after you." [51]

That's you and me.

Part of waking up is seeing Jesus for who He really is...right now. It's this Jesus who we are scheduled to meet in the sky.

Oh, and one more thing. To those who read His Revelation words aloud, a special blessing is promised. [52] It's the only book of the Bible that makes such a promise, with an additional blessing to the one who hears what it says and takes it to heart in obedience.

But why would He say this? Why is this so critical?

"Because," John writes, "the time is near." [53]

3

Wedding Dress

Something incredible happened a few centuries ago. A cultural upheaval. A revolution of sorts. But not the kind where kings and emperors die by assassination from angry peasants or trusted confidants. This was something more consequential, and exponentially greater.

What altered the trajectory of mankind's self-orbit all those years ago was supernatural. But surprisingly, what we discover at the epicenter of this global phenomenon is nothing more than a small group of ordinary people. Average guys and girls. Common folks coming together for a common purpose.

So what exactly was this occurrence that redefined humanity and wrote history itself?

It was the birth of the church.

Around AD 30, a spiritual revival began in an obscure upper room somewhere in Jerusalem. The body of Christ today traces its ancestry back to this insignificant band of soul brothers and sisters who launched a worldwide movement. Beginning with about a hundred believers, the early church's impact on society produced concentric circles of transformation that have continued expanding for two thousand years.

Currently, Christianity claims 2.1 billion followers. Not bad for a tiny Middle Eastern house church, huh?

But what did those first generation Christians possess that was so worth exporting to the ends of the earth? How did unremarkable people—without wealth, corporate connections, cultural influence, a church planting manual, or even a business plan—birth an international faith movement that shook the world?

In short, those spiritual trailblazers simply embraced the challenge given to them by their Lord. Taking ownership of their faith, theirs became an epic, supernatural story. And the same spirit and power that launched that movement is still around for any today who follow Christ and His plan.

But something happened to those believers along the way. Over time the dream began to slowly fade. The bride Jesus courted and won with love gradually drifted, losing herself in a difficult and confusing world.

In just two short generations, the church of Jesus found herself in deep trouble. So critical was her condition that Jesus felt it necessary to personally address a series of sobering letters to her. In those messages, the Son of God rebukes several key congregations, calling them back to where they once belonged. In doing so, He sounds an alarm awaking His bride and alerting her to His imminent return.

Twenty centuries later, His words still ring true. Words meant to rouse God's church from a stupefying slumber, to change and challenge her (and us) to re-envision the church. In the pages of John's Revelation, Jesus Himself calls us back to the original spirit of Christianity.

The Unplugged Generation

From the time he was old enough to walk, my son Clayton destroyed things. He took apart his toys (and sometimes his brothers' toys), often demolishing them for no other reason than to see how they were made and what made them work. Once satisfied, he would either put them back together again or create some kind of hybrid—like the time he made a flashlight out of spare parts from a toy race car. I expected to come home one day to discover he had assembled a space shuttle out of kitchen appliances.

Then we heard about a local youth program run by a retired engineer. This older gentleman loved to help teenage boys build things from scratch and come up with new and inventive ways of understanding how stuff works. Appropriately called Project Lab, this club gave a dozen or so young men the chance to do what they loved most—tear stuff up, experiment with the parts (sometimes on each other), and then create magical machines out of them.

I'll never forget that night following Clayton's initial visit to Project Lab. Racing up to the car, wild-eyed and with a huge grin across his fourteen-year-old face, he exclaimed, "Mom! Dad! You won't believe this. There are other kids out there *just like me.*"

Maybe you know how he feels.

As a believer in Jesus, perhaps you've felt like an oddball at times. Like you didn't belong. But I'm not talking about the feeling you get out there "in the world." I'm referring to that feeling you get on Sundays. To be blunt, *you don't like church.*

And I know how you feel. Actually, people have a lot of reasons for not liking church—some of them legit and some not. Some people are never satisfied with anything in life. They're always complaining about something, and church is just another casualty in their cross fire. Others are unconventional in their thinking and the way God is presented in church is unstimulating to them. Creative personalities often struggle with boredom and predictability with church, while others can't seem to pay attention for any length of time. Some people are looking for the perfect church, a guaranteed fruitless search.

I've met a lot of people who've left the church to pursue some other kind of Christian experience, and many who have no intentions of ever returning to what they see as a "corporate religious institution." They're repulsed by opulent multimillion dollar facilities while those in their community (even fellow Christians) suffer.

There may be truth in some or all of these claims. However, I've wondered if this massive disconnect is more due to the fact that Christians and churches have collectively drifted from Jesus's original vision for His "called out ones."[1] Maybe all of us share a portion of the responsibility here. Churches are made up of people, and people are flawed. Sometimes a church's vision of what it should be and how it should operate is ineffective and irrelevant. I know churches that try way too hard to be hip and edgy. At the same time, many are awesome and effective, even though no one church is stellar in every area. No church can be everything to everyone.

But one thing I am sure of—something deep within the spirit of redeemed believers (both in and outside the church) is crying out for the real thing, something Jesus envisioned from the very beginning.

So what about you? Have you ever wished your Sunday experience could be more?

Ever wanted to make a more meaningful connection with God in the context of your church?

Ever wished you could go beyond the shallow relationships (often falsely called "fellowship") and really start doing life with a group of people?

Do you find yourself forgetting the point of the pastor's message before you get home? Or worse, do you exit church each week under a gray cloud of guilt because you're not a better Christian?

Have you ever wished people could just be themselves at church, forgetting the formalities and fake conversations?

Ever wished your church could be more of a gathering of ordinary people instead of concert venues and stage performances?

Ever wondered if there were others out there just like you?

Instead of lobbing grenades of criticism at the church, Scripture's solution to our struggle involves rediscovering the original beauty of Christ and His beautiful bride.

If that's what you seek, then you're in luck, because that's exactly what Jesus wants you and your church to do.

In order to understand how to live in the present and prepare ourselves for what's coming, we as the church must first know who we are and where we've come from. Revelation 2 and 3 help us do just that.

In these two short chapters, we discover that Jesus was deeply concerned about the state of His church at the close of the first century. And for good reason. On the whole, her condition was not good. She had gone missing, spiritually. And Jesus wanted her back. The church today is still His bride, and He loves her very much. And through His evaluation of first-century churches, we see a mirror image of ourselves and where we too fall short of His beautiful blueprint. More importantly, we understand how we can be a part of the solution in helping His church return to the original power and vision that changed history.

And in doing so, we effectively prepare ourselves to meet our now glorified bridegroom.

Flat Church

Our Christian culture talks a lot about a personal relationship with Jesus. That's really important, especially in a time when God is often viewed as impersonal or uncaring. This concept helps people see Christ's relevancy to their everyday lives. But as we look at the writings of Paul and John to first-century congregations, we see that Christianity is more than just a personal relationship with Jesus. According to Scripture, there's something else and something more.

We discover Jesus also has a personal relationship with churches, the collective group of believers in a local congregation. In fact, Paul wrote primarily to churches, not individuals.[2] This is one reason why identifying with a specific church is so critical. Calling a church "yours" puts you in a special relationship with Christ beyond your personal connection with Him. This not only gives

you encouragement and ministry opportunity, but also appropriate accountability. Though each of us is unique and fulfills a special
role in the body, we all wear the same team jersey. We're united, con-
nected via our spiritual DNA to a common body.[3]

So Jesus gives John the apostle seven distinct messages for seven
specific congregations of Christians. We could easily spend a chapter on each of these, and they're all worthy of our study. We could
talk about the Ephesian church, believers who had lost their original love for Christ. Or we could look at a small church, like the one
at Smyrna that may have had fewer than a hundred members.[4] And
yet Jesus told this tiny church that they were "rich" because of their
faithfulness to Him, even in the midst of intense persecution.

But of these seven churches in Revelation 2 and 3, let's focus on
just one of them—the church at Laodicea.

The city of Laodicea was located in the Lycus River Valley,
between the cities of Hierapolis and Colossae (to whom Paul wrote
Colossians). In fact the three were considered "sister cities." And
although Jesus commends several of these Revelation churches, He
has virtually nothing good to say about the church at Laodicea.

Our Lord even begins His message to them with a rebuke: "I
know your deeds, that you are neither cold nor hot; I wish that you
were cold or hot. So because you are lukewarm, and neither hot nor
cold, I will spit you out of My mouth."[5]

This church had become so distasteful to God that it made Him
want to spew them out of His mouth. These Christians actually
made Him nauseated. He wanted to vomit them up. Harsh words.
But why would Jesus ever say something like that to His bride?
What could possibly motivate Him to feel this way?

To understand what Jesus meant, some background information
is helpful. Nearby sister cities Hierapolis and Colossae were well-
known for their hot springs and cold mountain water, respectively.
However, Laodicea's local streams and rivers there were inadequate
(dirty). Because of this, water had to be brought in from the other

two cities, accomplished through construction of a series of underground aqueducts. But the cold water from Colossae was no longer cold by the time it reached Laodicea. No longer refreshing or thirst quenching. And the hot water carried in these pipes from Hierapolis became full of chemicals, clogging up the pipes, so the water that eventually arrived in Laodicea was dirty, impure and undrinkable. In other words, it tasted gross.

The result of all this was that Laodiceans didn't have the healing, therapeutic hot waters of Hierapolis *or* the refreshing, cold mountain waters of Colossae. Their water was lukewarm, impure and totally unsuitable for consumption. And visitors to Laodicea who happened to take a drink of their water supply immediately spewed it out of their mouths onto the ground.

So Jesus's first rebuke to this church was that they were "neither hot nor cold," but rather lukewarm. Nobody likes a hot tub at room temperature water or warm drinking water on a hot day. In other words, these believers were no longer passionately committed. They were stuck in the middle. Spiritually flat. Sadly, they didn't even know it. Or care. And this kind of spiritual apathy made Jesus feel sick.

Christ had spoken of this kind of mediocrity before in Luke 14:28-35, telling a huge crowd that unless they were radically committed to Him, He wouldn't permit them to be His disciples. Because of who He is, Jesus requires supreme love and dedication from His followers. Anything less than this is unacceptable because it tells Him we don't know who we're following.

That's a big commitment, and precisely why He advised prospective followers to first "count the cost." He went on to say, "Salt is good, but if it loses its saltiness, how can it be made salty again? It is fit neither for the soil nor for the manure pile; it is thrown out. Whoever has ears to hear, let them hear." [6]

An uncommitted Christian is like unsalty salt. The two words don't go together. What's the point of tasteless salt or a Christian who is uncommitted? It doesn't make sense. It's an oxymoron, causing you to question its very purpose and reason for being.

Jesus says to the church at Laodicea, "You've lost the one thing that made you distinct. The *one thing* that made you who you are. Your passionate loyalty to Me has faded. It's almost disappeared completely. You stopped caring about My relationship to your church. Along the way, your commitment for Me cooled down, so much so that you've become lukewarm, like your water. You're not worthless, just useless. And nauseating to Me."

Can you even imagine Jesus saying that to your church? Or to *you*?

Clueless Christians

But the Lord isn't finished. He has yet another stinging rebuke for this church. The second reason He will spit them out of His mouth is: "You say, 'I am rich; I have acquired wealth and do not need a thing.' But you do not realize that you are wretched, pitiful, poor, blind and naked."[7]

Throughout His earthly ministry, Jesus Christ was the master communicator, using familiar stories and metaphors relevant to His culture and time. He understood that illustrating spiritual truth this way helps the hearer to clearly grasp the concept. He does the same thing here. Laodicea's three main sources of wealth were banking, production of wool, and medicines. They prospered in these three areas, bringing affluence to the city's inhabitants. But though these Christians considered themselves rich, Jesus says they were actually wretched and poor. They thought they were clothed, but Jesus says they were embarrassingly naked. They believed they had 20/20 vision, but Jesus says they were actually blind. In the dark. In short, they were nothing they thought they were, and instead were everything they despised.

They didn't even know that they didn't know.

Perhaps the saddest of all life commentaries is when everyone around a person can see their blatant faults, but that person is oblivious to them. That's a deadly combination of deception and blindness. Jesus had some sobering and somewhat sarcastic advice for this lukewarm, clueless church: "I advise you to buy from me gold refined by fire, that you may become rich; and white garments, that you may clothe yourself, and that the shame of your nakedness may not be revealed; and eye salve to anoint your eyes, that you may see."[8]

Christ knows the best gold is refined by fire, removing the impurities from it. "Get some pure gold," Jesus says. "The kind that comes from Me. Then you will truly become rich."

The Laodiceans were also known for their raven-black wool industry. Christ tells them to cover their nakedness and shame with the purity of His white wool (symbolizing righteousness). This church trusted in themselves and their own resources, and Jesus wanted them to transfer that trust to Him. Third, the medical school in Laodicea produced a healing eye salve, but Jesus offered them a heavenly eye salve that would restore their *spiritual* sight, enabling them to clearly see themselves and their condition. Only then would they understand reality and God's truth.

But though the Laodicean's pride, apathy, and self-absorption were sickening to God, He did not stop loving them. The very reason He was sending this message was because of His great love for them. Though they were faithless, He would remain faithful.[9] Faithful to love *and* discipline them.[10] Jesus hopes His words alone will be enough to awake this flatlining church so that they can keep their lampstand.[11]

"Knock, Knock…"

As with any of God's commands, there's always a choice for us to make. We each have a responsibility when God calls. Always something for us to think, believe, or do. And what is that something here? Jesus says the entire church should repent and let His words produce change in them.[12]

Pride can easily cause us to nod our heads in agreement at God's Word and yet not allow it to gain traction in our hearts and minds. Complacency is one of the Christian's worst enemies. Thinking we're something we're not and living mediocre, lukewarm spiritual lives puts us in danger of being rebuked and disciplined by Jesus. As believers we must take God seriously and take to heart His words of correction when they come. So listen carefully when His Spirit prompts you. Sometimes His rebuke comes directly from His Word. Other times from the Holy Spirit, our conscience, a pastor, friend, or even circumstances. Then we must make the decision to change our minds so God can change the way we live. That's what Jesus means by *repent*.[13]

But there is also a huge benefit involved in turning back to Him this way. Jesus promises a special reward to the church that does what He asks of them. Actually, it's a twofold blessing, and He uses yet another word picture to help the bride He loves understand what's at stake here. Christ portrays Himself standing at the door of the church, knocking. "Behold, I stand at the door and knock; if *anyone* hears My voice and opens the door, I will come in to him, and will dine with him, and he with Me."[14]

How sad that Jesus should have to knock on the door of the very church that bears His name. And yet this illustrates once again the church's responsibility in the relationship. Jesus is not forcing Himself on us. He politely but authoritatively knocks, calling out to His bride inside. He only asks for one believer to open that symbolic church door. Just *one* church member confessing their foolish pride and repenting is all it would take for Jesus to reenter their congregation.

And if they open the door, what happens then? The Lord promises to "dine" with them. In first-century Middle Eastern culture, the evening meal was a time when family and close friends came together. Rather than sit at tables like we do, they reclined on cushions and often right beside each other.[15] Their physical closeness during supper mirrored a relational closeness. Dinner was a time of fellowship, transparency, and intimacy. Even today, we have lunch or dinner with someone as a way to get to know them better or just to spend time with someone we love.

"You want to be close to Me again?" Jesus announces. "Like it used to be? Then open this door (repent), invite Me in, and let's have dinner together." Christianity is indeed about a personal relationship, and that's exactly what Jesus desires with every church and every member of that church.

Is that what you truly desire? To be with Jesus in close fellowship?

Christ says a second benefit to repenting is that it enables those who "overcome" to "sit down with Me on My throne."[16] Every true Christian is an overcomer by nature.[17] And the reward for persevering with Christ is that we'll share in some of His heavenly privileges and authority when we reign with Him.[18] "Overcome this crippling disease of yours," He says, "and I promise to honor you."

What genuine Christian would choose a self-centered lifestyle of mediocre, apathetic lukewarmness when they can dine with the Lord every day, overcome, and look forward to unimaginable heavenly rewards?

Is this a no-brainer, or does it reveal something of the incredible deceptive power of sin?

Romancing the Stone Heart

So how does a church like the one at Laodicea devolve into a congregation of mediocre ministries, boring Bible studies, and a lack of passionate love for Jesus?

How could a group of Christians ever motivate Jesus to declare, "Hey, sorry, but I can't use you anymore. You're officially unusable. No good to Me or My kingdom. I'm benching you"?

And what does this kind of unappetizing lukewarmness really look like in our lives? How does a believer become lukewarm over time? How would you know if you're "living in Laodicea"? Jesus says, "You know you're lukewarm when…

- you no longer require My help to make it through your day."
- you aren't desperate for Me like you used to be."
- you can 'do church' without Me. I could leave the building and you wouldn't even know it."
- you surround yourself with things and people who take your love and attention away from Me."
- you consistently ignore the promptings of My Holy Spirit."
- you have no idea how spiritually destitute, bankrupt, empty, blind, and naked you have become."
- you fail to live with an awareness of your own sinfulness."
- you lose the passion to worship and be with My people" (Hebrews 10:23-25).
- you've lost the overflowing gratitude that comes from being forgiven" (2 Peter 1:9; Romans 8:1).
- your hunger for obeying My truth wanes" (John 14:15; 1 Peter 2:2-3).
- you can attend church without experiencing Me."
- you no longer care to influence others for Me."

Those are some serious spiritual indictments. But people who love their God and church think about such things.

And if individual Christians become lukewarm, entire churches do as well. So how does a local church in the latter days guard herself from becoming lukewarm and thus nauseating to God? Here are a few warning signs:

- Functioning like "nickels and noses" are what's most important. Money and church growth drive the ministry.

- Obsession over trivial things, often labeled "pursuing excellence." ("Should we go for a ten- or twenty-second transition between worship songs?")

- Neglecting corporate prayer and an attitude of desperate dependence on God. Using prayer as an afterthought or ritual to get God's blessing.

- Relying on programs, personality, natural talent, spiritual giftedness, and material resources over reliance on the Holy Spirit.

Churches today can easily mistake busyness, meetings, activities, innovative programs, and multiple ministries for being a healthy body. And though doctrine is very important, believing the right things isn't the only way to measure our approval rating with God. Jesus never faulted churches for believing in orthodox truth. But true theology should always naturally lead to collective love for the Lord Jesus Christ. Orthodoxy without passionate love for Jesus makes a church lukewarm at worst and an ecclesiastical classroom at best.

Fervent commitment is what Jesus is looking for in His bride. That quality literally defines who we are.

I believe He still "walks among the lampstands" asking, "Is your church really committed to Me?" He's still knocking on doors.

Many Christians and churches today are in danger of losing the one thing that sets them apart. Churches are neither religious institutions nor organizations. Christ's body is instead a beautiful living *organism* whose unique calling is her first-love devotion to Jesus Christ. That's what's missing. That was the original vision and pioneer spirit of Jesus's church. We know the early church had plenty of faults, but there's no denying that we are a far cry from what we once were. Over time we have become tame. Domesticated. We have become institutions and businesses. We value numbers over knowing God. Buildings over building up people. Entertainment over engaging the person of Christ. Activity over actively pursuing Him.

And God is bored with it all.

He yawns at our cutting-edge services and shakes His head at our full calendars. He grieves when we think our church is better than others because we're big and wealthy or because we create multisite campuses, do more in the community, or find ministry in some third world country.

But what really gets His attention, what raises His heartbeat, what gives His Spirit pleasure beyond description is when God's people respond to His Son with fervent, fanatical, loving commitment. Strip everything else away and what's left? Radical love for Jesus is what births programs and ministries, not vice versa. And it's what attracts people to God. Love *for* Jesus coming from truth *about* Jesus is a powerful combination.

What if you could actually see the lampstands of the churches in your city? To see with God's eyes the amount of actual light each local church shines? To be able to know and discern the real kingdom influence and disciplemaking effect each church has? What if we measured success the way God does? What if the amount of light emanating from each church was directly proportionate to the *love* that church has for Jesus Christ?

Oh, to be a bride madly in love with a God who is madly in love with us!

Therefore, we must guard against Westernizing her. Americanizing her. Politicizing her. Moralizing her. Modernizing her. Glamorizing her. Segregating her. And by doing so, compromising her.

I believe God is searching for believers, in or out of church, who feel like religious robots. He's calling out to those who are bored with doing another church activity or attending a show on Sunday.

He is looking for people who want to really know Him and not just go through the motions of going to church.

Pastor A.W. Tozer once said, "If the Holy Spirit was withdrawn from the church today, 95 percent of what we do would go on and no one would know the difference. If the Holy Spirit had been withdrawn from the New Testament church, 95 percent of what they did would stop, and everybody would know the difference."

Does the church really need God anymore? Or can we do this without Him? The Laodiceans apparently thought they could.

We have to once again believe God is necessary for our church, and that packed auditoriums, cutting-edge presentations, and professionally produced Sunday services are not enough to conjure Him up. Jesus is calling His church—corporately and individually—to repent and return to a simplicity and purity of devotion to Him.[19]

You, my friend, are a part of that solution. You can rebel or withdraw from an imperfect church or you can lend a hand and help out by being an "on fire" believer. I believe our Father is calling a new generation of disciples back to Him. Back to the way He intended the body of Christ to be. Back to His original plan.

Travel to Laodicea today and all you'll find are rubble and ruins. But far worse than their landscape is their legacy. Jesus didn't care about their banks, wool, or medical school. He cared about *her*— the apple of His eye. The love of His heart. The church. His bride.

As we prepare ourselves for the return of the bridegroom, we must guard ourselves from living like lukewarm Laodiceans. Instead, let's clothe ourselves with the Wedding Dress of pure love for Him.

Jesus is still knocking on church doors today. In calling His bride *out*, He's calling her *up* to something better. His original idea for the church is as good today as it was when His Spirit first birthed her in that upper room. Through our passionate, loving commitment to Him we can bring the present-day church full circle, back to the revolutionary, classic beauty of vintage Christianity.

Are you in?

4

Grounding the Rapture

Jesus Christ is coming back.

For the vast majority of Christians, there is no question or controversy about that. The real questions are how and when? And among respected theologians and biblical scholars, there's divergence of opinion about this climactic event. At its core, the issue seems to be, "Is what we have come to know as the Rapture legit or not?" Is it some lame first-century science fiction or cheesy end-times scare tactic? Or is it an apocalyptic-launching reality from God Himself?

The answer to this question is of monumental importance. If the events depicted in Revelation 6–19 are still future, and if there is no Rapture, then believers are destined to endure the horrible judgments and plagues God sends upon the earth during the seven-year period known as the Great Tribulation. So it is not a belief to be easily dismissed or taken lightly.

What's the Big Deal?

If you've been paying attention, you've noticed that the Rapture's reputation has suffered somewhat in recent years. You could blame this recent ridicule on low-budget movies or campy Christian novels. Visual or verbal depictions of millions disappearing from the earth (and the resulting panic and chaos) have become relatively easy marketing tools for book publishers and movie producers. That's because, along with sex, *fear* also does pretty well at the box office and bookstore.

But if we've learned anything recently, it's that blockbuster movies and bestselling books tend to embellish biblical truth for effect and shock value. This has been the case with stories depicting Noah and Moses. But it's especially true when it comes to the end times. Specifically, the Rapture has been typically portrayed in B-rated movies with sub-par production and acting. So in one sense, the modern approach to the Rapture has become the Rapture's own worst enemy. And while criticisms over recent portrayals of this event may very well be deserved, the question remains, "Is there really such a future event foretold by Scripture, and if so, what does God say about it? What can we know for sure?"

There's a flow of thought these days that permeates postmodern Christian reasoning. It goes something like this: "You can't be 100 percent sure of X doctrine, and it really doesn't matter anyway." Assertions about absolute truth, and particularly about anything related to prophecy, are deemed invalid since no one knows the future, right? Plus, the spirit of the age dictates that we display immediate skepticism against any form of spiritual dogma. Being confident regarding God's truth is often considered arrogant, narrow-minded, old school, unenlightened, and even mean-spirited. And this attitude exists not only in the secular world, but within the Christian community as well.

A new millennial generation of atheists and professing Christians share an aversion toward definitive (or what they consider to be exclusive) beliefs. They often unite over redefining and even rejecting long-held Christian orthodoxy—such as the verbal inspiration and inerrancy of the Bible, a literal interpretation of the Genesis creation account, biblical gender roles, and even basic sexuality as described in Scripture. These historic biblical truths have become fair game for "emerging theologians" to reinterpret in order to make the Bible and its archaic teachings fit more comfortably into mainstream culture and its evolving morality. So it comes as no surprise that when the doctrine of the Rapture is taught or strongly believed, it is dismissed by some as invalid and passé.

All this has created what theologian Charles Ryrie once called "eschatological agnosticism." It's the sentiment that says, "Since I don't know, you can't either."

But can those who promote doctrinal *un*certainty be sure of their uncertainty? Can they be dogmatic about their professed ignorance? Do those who consider themselves to be true skeptics ever question their own skepticism? Or do they simply become just like those they accuse of being narrow-minded?

All of the previously mentioned biblical doctrines and truths have great significance, relevance, and real-life implications. In other words, all doctrine really does matter...especially if it's true!

Think of it this way. Wouldn't you want to know whether you'll suffer unimaginable judgments, persecution, plagues, famine, demonic infestation, economic disaster, world wars, and probable death through beheading? If there is a future Rapture, wouldn't you want to embrace that reality just as you do all other important Bible truths?

I would hope so!

That principle alone makes the Rapture an important subject worth investigating. God specifically stated that He did not want us to be ignorant about this truth, unlike unbelievers who don't even care. Paul even equated believing in the "coming of the Lord" with believing in the resurrection.[1] So according to him, it really is a big deal.

Rebuffing, Ridiculing, and Removing the Rapture

But not everyone believes in the Rapture, and for reasons they see as convincing. So let's look at some of them.

The *first* common objection to the Rapture is that the word itself is not even in the Bible. And that's true. Search your Bible from Genesis to Revelation, and you won't find the word *rapture* anywhere. But in that same search, you'll also never find the words *trinity, missions, great commission, Easter, incarnation,* or *monotheism.* The word *Christian* appears only three times. Even the word *bible* isn't in the Bible. And yet, from the first century until now, Christians have believed in all these core beliefs firmly rooted in Scripture and established in the early church. Had you asked one of the Ephesian Christians if she believed in the trinity, you'd have been met with a blank stare. The word *trinity* was coined later as a helpful way of describing a truth clearly taught in the Bible. Words or phrases like these simply enable us to understand and remember the biblical truths they represent. Therefore, the argument that the word *rapture* is not even in the Bible doesn't disprove the Rapture.

So if the word itself is not in the Bible, where does this belief in rapture come from? Our English word stems from a transliteration of the Latin word *rapturo.* When translating 1 Thessalonians 4:17 from Greek into Latin in the fourth century, the Catholic Church translated the Greek word describing this event as *rapiemur,* a form of the verb *rapio.*[2] Over time, another form of the word (*rapturo*) was used when speaking of the truth contained in this verse. Our English word *rapture* is derived from this Latin word.

However, what's immensely more important than what English or Latin words we use is the meaning of the original Greek verb and how it is used in its context. It really doesn't matter whether we call a particular spring Sunday Easter, Resurrection Day, Rise Up Sunday, or Empty Tomb Day. What matters is if there actually was a resurrection, right?

The Greek word used in Scripture to describe the Rapture means to "suddenly snatch away." So we could just as easily refer to this truth as the "catching up," the "disappearance," or the "snatching away" (though these aren't nearly as memorable).

Second, some dismiss the Rapture by arguing that Christians are like the people of Israel, whom God protected from harm in the midst of the ten plagues He unleashed on Pharaoh and Egypt. The people weren't delivered *out* of the plagues but rather exempted *from* them. And yet nowhere in Revelation or anywhere else in Scripture does God state there exists this parallel protection between Israel and the church. Further, those who come to faith during the Tribulation receive no "exemption clause" from John. There is nothing to indicate that they will be given some invisible umbrella of protection from all of God's awful judgments. In fact, John implies quite the opposite when describing the redeemed multitude who suffer and die during that seven-year period, saying "they will hunger no longer, neither thirst anymore; nor will the sun beat down on them, nor any heat...and God will wipe every tear from their eyes."[3]

So it's clear that those who become believers during the Tribulation will suffer greatly as God's rain of wrath falls on both the just and the unjust. That would seem to be an additional wise motivation to trust in Christ *before* that terrible time comes upon the earth.

Third, others discard the idea of the Rapture because it appears to be a truth conveniently created, giving Christians a way out of the horrible events of the tribulation period, as if we think we're more privileged than our spiritual ancestors who endured suffering and persecution. But if we're really paying attention to what is currently happening to believers worldwide, it's clear that being a Christian isn't getting any easier as we ramp up to Revelation.

Besides, believing the Rapture in no way suggests that Christians are currently immune from hardship, prejudice, persecution, or even martyrdom. On the contrary, all evidence points to a continued, increasing hostility toward Jesus and His followers as Satan stokes the white-hot fires of hatred in the last days.

I believe there will be plenty of tribulation to go around for true believers in the time leading up to the Tribulation. The truth of the Rapture simply means we miss God's future judgments on an unbelieving world during the Tribulation. Actually, it's very likely Christians will be persecuted and martyred, possibly resembling first-century Roman oppression, in the days leading up to the events depicted in Revelation. Put another way, never in history has there been a Tribulation leading to Armageddon. It's a day unlike any other, an unparalleled period of time. Nothing compares to it.

So if a deliverance of believers prior to future wrath exists, it is no more a convenient escape clause than were the deliverances of Noah, Lot, or Rahab—all delivered *before* God's judgment fell. Nowhere in Scripture does God promise to exempt believers from all suffering, trials, or persecution (John 16:1-3; Romans 8:33-36). History is proof of this. However, the Tribulation is not primarily about Christian suffering and persecution, but about God's angry wrath upon unbelieving humanity. And Scripture specifically assures us we are exempt from this anger and wrath, for why would Jesus punish His beloved bride prior to taking her to heaven?[4]

Those who trust in Christ are delivered from God's wrath against sin (demonstrated at the cross) and God's wrath against sinners (demonstrated during the Tribulation). Further, God's sovereign prerogative allows Him to do as He pleases, and if He chooses to rescue the righteous prior to judgment, why should any true believer have a problem with that?[5]

Fourth, it's also become trendy today to claim that only in the last few hundred years has the idea of the Rapture existed, and that historically the church hasn't believed in such a doctrine. Some claim the Rapture suddenly appeared on our spiritual radar, bursting onto the scene as something new to Scripture, novel to us, and nonexistent in church history. But is this really the case?

We have to begin by reminding ourselves of a few essential facts:

1. *Whether a particular doctrine or belief is dominant throughout all of church history is not always a reliable factor in determining its validity.* Salvation by grace through faith, a doctrine clearly taught by Paul and attacked by many in the early church, suffered greatly for centuries during the dominance of the Catholic Church. However, it came bursting back to the forefront of Christian theology around 1518 with Martin Luther's *Ninety-Five Theses.*[6] Arguments that the Bible is without error have received far greater attention in the last 150 years than perhaps the previous nineteen centuries combined. In many denominations, the debate is still going on, but you wouldn't conclude based on that that it is some sort of "new teaching."

Regarding the Rapture, you may be surprised to know that belief in a pretribulational deliverance can be found in church history as early as the fourth century.[7] Further, *The Didache*, a first-century document, also considered the Lord's coming as an event that could occur at any time.[8] The early church fathers (first and second centuries) and later the Reformers often linked the events of the Great Tribulation with contemporary events of their day, therefore maintaining the same spirit of expectancy.[9] So to argue that belief in the Rapture is a recent idea is historically unsupportable. The logic to uphold such an argument simply isn't there. As we'll see in the following chapter, an imminent Rapture has been a core belief of Christians since the first century.

2. *The articulation and understanding of many historic Christian beliefs have been refined over the past two thousand years.* This is both a natural and necessary process. Some of these doctrinal refinements have come about due to the rise of heretical beliefs and practices. For example, because of the Judaizers' false teachings, Paul was forced to confront and correct their heresy, and in the process greatly clarified the doctrines of grace and liberty for the Galatians (and for Peter). In the second century, a bishop's son named Marcion became known

in the church at Rome for rejecting the God of the Old Testament because of His wrath. Marcion excluded from his personal teaching anything perceived as negative (i.e., hell and judgment), believing these things didn't belong in Scripture. As a result, he was soundly condemned by the church fathers.[10]

Baptismal regeneration (the belief that baptism assists salvation and cleansing from sin) also crept into the church through apocryphal writings (*Epistle of Barnabas, Shepherd of Hermas*) and even in some of the church fathers themselves.[11] This continued with the Catholic Church throughout the Middle Ages. This was another reason that motivated Martin Luther to try to reform the Church. But the Church refused, forcing Luther to break away, choosing biblical truth over Catholic tradition. Over time, others joined him and the purity of the church was rescued. This had to happen so that future generations would not mistake what salvation was all about.

So it is not surprising that throughout the church's messy history, certain interpretations of Scripture and doctrine could be described as "recent" in the context of their day. However, none of these are considered to be new revelation, but instead provide a more complete understanding of existing biblical revelation and prophetic passages. We should never legitimize those who claim they've discovered something in the Bible no one else in two thousand years has ever seen, such as the date for Jesus's return, new revelation about heaven, or some hidden Bible code.

Therefore, some core beliefs were tested in the first few hundred years of Christianity, while other doctrines have been made clearer and our understanding of them refined over time because of conflict, heresy, and a growing, comprehensive grasp of theology.

3. Prophecy (into whose category the Rapture falls) by its very nature often begins with great mystery, unveiling itself gradually (or sometimes all at once) with a particular event or series of signs.[12] A few hundred years ago, virtually no one could have envisioned the rebirth of Israel and the return of Jews worldwide to the land God had previously given to them. But this happened in 1948, giving us fresh insight into Scriptures that for centuries were mysterious in their potential fulfillment.[13] The existence and rebirth of Israel is considered an undeniable affirmation of biblical prophecy. That's something we didn't know just seventy-five years ago.

Further, up until the last few decades, no one could have imagined how a single world leader could require every inhabitant on the planet to bear a mark identifying them as a worshipper of this man and an eligible participant in his last-days economy. But with the recent dissolution of international economic borders and more nations coming together for mutual survival, the possibility and technology for such a mark are now here. Right now. (More about this in chapter 10.)

In every case, the test of any claimed prophetic fulfillment or understanding of doctrine is to hold it up to the light of Scripture. The ultimate question is always and forever, "What does the Bible say?"

Historically, the church has not paid a huge amount of attention to apocalyptic prophecy until modern times, when the fulfillment of those prophecies began to seem more viable. To question whether the Rapture is a dominant subject throughout every stage of church history is insufficient for determining the Rapture's validity as several other important doctrines have also been intermittently highlighted at different times.

So we can see that these popular attacks on the Rapture aren't sufficient to cast serious doubt on this important doctrine. We have to appeal to a higher authority than human emotion, theological tradition, personal objection, or opinion.[14] Instead, we ask, "Is it taught in the Word of God? Is the Rapture actually a part of New Testament teaching? And what does it really mean for you, the bride?"

5

The Bridegroom Comes!

There's a bizarre scene described in Revelation this way,

> And they said to the mountains and the rocks, "Fall on us and hide us from the presence of Him who sits on the throne, and from the wrath of the Lamb; for the great day of their wrath has come, and who is able to stand?"[1]

This depicts the reactions of unbelievers to the first round of judgments as God begins pouring out His wrath upon the earth in a future seven year period known as the "Tribulation." But if these and other events described in Revelation 6–19 are merely metaphoric or symbolic (as some claim), then it becomes virtually impossible to figure out what God was thinking when He gave this wild Revelation to John. In which case, it's anyone's guess what it actually means or what purpose it serves in Scripture.[2]

If, however, it means what it appears to say and can be interpreted literally, then the real question becomes, "Will the bride of Christ be subjected to this hell on earth for seven years, or will she be rescued prior to it?"[3] Is Jesus currently preparing and purifying His bride in order to deliver her from the Tribulation and to join Him in heaven? Or is He simply getting her ready to endure the divine wrath of God (and Satan) during that period of time? If the answer to the first question is yes, then the church *must* be absent from the Tribulation and by necessity be taken up prior to it.

Wrath or Rescue?

Several key Bible passages speak directly to this.[4]

In His message to the church in Philadelphia, Jesus promises, "I also will keep you from the hour of testing, that hour which is about to come upon the whole world, to test those who dwell on the earth."[5] We've already established that the seven churches of Revelation 2–3 foreshadow the church in the last days.[6] Here, Jesus Christ pledges to keep the church *from* the "hour of testing" (contextually here, the Tribulation period). There's a world of difference between being kept *in* trials and being kept *from* them. In John 12:23, Jesus speaks about the "hour" (or time period) of His suffering and death. A few verses later, He confesses, "My soul has become troubled; and what shall I say, 'Father, save Me *from* this hour'? But for this purpose I came to this hour." To be kept from that hour would've meant Jesus avoids the cross completely, meaning He's delivered from that suffering, missing it altogether.

But clearly, God did not deliver Him from that hour. However, here in Revelation 3, He does promise to save His church *from* the great day of His wrath. Think of it this way: If God merely protected (kept) us during His Tribulation wrath, we would miss the judgments but still live through that period of time. If you live *through* a period of time, you can still miss some of the events of that time. But if you miss the entire time period (kept *from* the hour) you miss all the events!

While living on the Gulf Coast for five years, our family survived several fierce hurricanes. One of them was Hurricane Danny in 1997, which caused more than a $100 million in damages, dropping a record amount of rainfall. To say we "rode out" that storm means we were kept *in* or *through* the hour of the storm. But if we evacuated and left town, we would be kept *from* the storm, missing it completely.

Further, the church as described in the New Testament is not mentioned once in Revelation 4–18. The word *church* or *churches* (Greek, *ekklesia*) is found twenty times in the book of Revelation. Nineteen of those references are in Revelation 1–3 and one is in Revelation 22. But there is zero mention of the church for fifteen chapters, during the time God unleashes His wrath. Not until chapter 19 do we see the bride reappearing on the scene, coming *from heaven.* This is compelling evidence for the church's absence during the Tribulation and further confirmation of the Rapture. Jesus promises to keep the church *from* the hour of Tribulation.

Wedding, Not Wrath

But long before the Lord spoke those words to the Philadelphian church, He gave a prior promise to Revelation's author and eleven of His friends. The disciples' world was about to come crashing down before their eyes. In a matter of hours, they would be rocked with shock and awe and their faith all but dismantled as their Lord would be arrested, beaten, scourged, stripped, and nailed to a crude wooden beam. Jesus prepared them for this traumatic experience by giving them a vision of hope for the future. They were in need of some big-time, tangible reassurance that He was not abandoning them forever. They desperately needed some comfort, and a promise that everything was going to work out somehow in the end. Earlier, Jesus had rebuked the Pharisees because though they were filled with religious thoughts, they could not understand the signs of the times. Christ told them to stop looking for signs and to start trusting His Word.[7] That's why He now speaks these prophetic words of assurance to His men.

> "Do not let your hearts be troubled. You believe in God; believe also in me. My Father's house has many rooms; if

that were not so, would I have told you that I am going
there to prepare a place for you? And if I go and prepare
a place for you, I will come back and take you to be with
me that you also may be where I am."[8]

Looking into eyes longing for good news, Jesus speaks of His
soon departure from earth. In doing so, He chooses His words carefully, using a familiar metaphor that calls to their mind the customs
surrounding Jewish weddings of the day. This unique wedding culture was a well-known way of life for the Jewish community, and
one that some of his men had personally experienced. Jesus even
chose to perform His first public miracle at a Jewish wedding.[9]

Part of this wedding tradition was that couples would be
engaged up to twenty-four months before their actual wedding day.
(No Vegas weddings back then!) Typically, the father of the groom
arranged the match.[10] The groom-to-be delivered detailed intentions for marriage in a written covenant (called a *ketubah*), which
he delivered to his future bride and her father. He also presented the
father with a gift—a symbol of compensation for the cost of raising
her. Once accepted, the man offered a cup of wine to the girl (representing a blood covenant). Drinking the cup meant acceptance of
the proposal and the beginning of the betrothal period. The woman
spent the following months during her engagement making herself ready and guarding her purity for her husband. She would even
wear a veil in public, signifying that she was spoken for (or "bought
with a price").[11]

Their engagement was considered legally binding, to the extent
that the betrothed couple even paid taxes together. This extended
betrothal period served several purposes:

1. It allowed time to make wedding plans.

2. It provided sufficient opportunity to demonstrate that
   the woman was not pregnant. In the event this was

discovered, the man could break the engagement, but only through a legal letter of divorce.[12]

3. During the engagement period, the groom returned to his father's house where he would spend months *preparing a place* for him and his bride to live following the wedding.

The woman's hope for her wedding day rested solely on the man's promise to come and claim her at an appointed time. Then, on the day of their wedding, the groomsmen arrived at the bride's house, shouting and sounding the shofar.[13] The groom then "snatched his bride up," taking her to his father's house where the couple consummated the marriage. Then all the wedding guests partied for seven days!

Jesus and His Jewish friends were familiar with all these wedding customs. And that knowledge was the backdrop of His words to them on their final night together. This included a solemn vow to return unexpectedly and snatch them away one day. In light of this background, let's again hear Jesus's words:

> "Do not let your hearts be troubled. You believe in God; believe also in me. *My Father's house* has many *rooms*; if that were not so, would I have told you that I am going there to *prepare a place for you*? And if I go and prepare a place for you, *I will come back and take you to be with me* that you also may be where I am."[14]

If there is no gathering up (Rapture) of the bride, why would Jesus use such a powerful and familiar engagement/wedding metaphor to mirror His return for us? That would send a confusing message, essentially misleading His followers. He even prefaces this wedding illustration with strong words: "You believe in God; believe also in me."

Jesus is saying, "Men, count on Me just like you count on God.

You have My word on this." Jesus's promise to return for His bride is inseparably linked to His own character. His integrity is at stake here.

Paul also used this bridal imagery when teaching about the church and her relationship to Jesus. He even describes her as a virgin waiting to be presented to her bridegroom.[15]

I've performed many weddings over the years, and in every case there is an exuberant expectation on the part of the bride leading up to her special day. Unfortunately, the church today has lost her anticipation for her bridegroom's arrival. Her heart doesn't beat faster when we speak about that glorious, joyous day.

It's this same bridal spirit of expectation and excitement that prompted Paul to write, "looking for the blessed hope and the appearing of the glory of our great God and Savior, Jesus Christ."[16]

The apostle John, present the night Jesus uttered His promise in John 14, later wrote regarding our preparation for Jesus's return, "We know that when He appears, we will be like Him, because we will see Him just as He is. And everyone who has this hope fixed on Him purifies himself, just as He is pure."[17]

Jesus is the groom. We are His bride. And He is returning to snatch us away one day.

Defying Gravity

Perhaps the best-known passage regarding the Rapture is found in 1 Thessalonians 4:13-18. Paul's letters to the Thessalonian believers included quite a bit of teaching about the end times. Apparently they had lots of questions and confusion regarding the last days and the return of Christ.[18] In the first of his two letters, he praises the Thessalonians for turning from idols "to wait for His Son from heaven, whom He raised from the dead, that is Jesus, who rescues us from the wrath to come."[19] Later in that same letter, speaking of the "day of the Lord," Paul proclaims, "God has not destined us for wrath, but for obtaining salvation through our Lord Jesus Christ."[20]

The context of this passage is not eternity (heaven and hell) but rather the *last days*. Paul had just written in the previous verses,

> But we do not want you to be uninformed, brethren, about those who are asleep, so that you will not grieve as do the rest who have no hope. For if we believe that Jesus died and rose again, even so God will bring with Him those who have fallen asleep in Jesus. For this we say to you by the word of the Lord, that we who are alive and remain until the coming of the Lord, will not precede those who have fallen asleep. For the Lord Himself will descend from heaven with a shout, with the voice of the archangel and with the trumpet of God, and the dead in Christ will rise first. Then we who are alive and remain will be caught up together with them in the clouds to meet the Lord in the air, and so we shall always be with the Lord.[21]

It was important to Paul that these believers be equipped with knowledge and clarity concerning Christ's return for them. Ignorance creates despair and confusion, draining hope, so Paul here sets the record straight. The Thessalonian Christians were expecting Jesus to come back at any time, and so they were worried about what happens to those Christians who have already died ("fallen asleep"), whether they will miss out on the Lord's return. The apostle reassures them that the spirits of those who have died in Christ will return with Him when He comes. He then unpacks the actual *chronology* of the Lord's arrival.

First, Jesus personally descends from heaven, accompanied by a "shout." He will cry out with a loud voice, perhaps as He did in calling Lazarus out of the grave.[22] But what will He say? Will He beckon to His beloved, "Bride, come forth!"? No one knows. However, we can be certain of four things:

1. It will be loud.

2. It will be heard by every believer on the entire planet.

3. It will unquestionably be the authoritative voice of God.

4. It will be the summons of a bridegroom calling His
   bride to the wedding.

Second, Jesus's shout will be immediately followed by another voice, that of the archangel. This class of angel is unique and possesses great authority and responsibility among the angelic host. Scripture reveals only one archangel's name—Michael.[23] However, there is evidence to suggest there are more like him, as he is called "one of the chief princes."[24] Michael's responsibilities include standing guard over Israel, waging war with Satan, and commanding authority over other angels.[25] So we don't know if this archangel is Michael or perhaps another one like him whose specific responsibility is to intervene on behalf of the church. In any event, this angel will also shout, perhaps a shout of triumph, or more likely heralding the arrival of the groom. In Jesus's parable of the ten virgins, Matthew records, "At midnight there was a shout, 'Behold, the bridegroom! Come out to meet him.'"[26]

Accompanying these unmistakable voices will be the "trumpet of God." Trumpets are not as common or familiar to our culture as they were in ancient times. In secular culture, these instruments were used to announce the arrival of a king. But in ancient Israel, the trumpet of God was blasted to summon His people to a gathering.[27] The idea here is that this trumpet gets your attention. There is a certain splendor and glory associated with trumpets. Something regal and majestic about them. Like trumpets inaugurating the opening ceremonies at the Olympics, there's an immediate burst of excitement and anticipation upon hearing them. Paul also wrote to the Corinthians about this same trumpet blast: "Behold, I tell you a mystery; we will not all sleep, but we will all be changed, in a moment, in the twinkling of an eye, at the last trumpet; for the trumpet will sound, and the dead will be raised imperishable, and we will be changed."[28]

Jesus shouting. The archangel announcing. The trumpet of God blasting. This is a dramatic moment in history. I can't wait!

Could there be *any* doubt as to the reality of this event? Every true follower of Christ living on earth will be captivated by this compelling chorus of sound.

But that's not all.

These announcements are followed by action, as Jesus performs a midair miracle, His first on-site in at least two thousand years. From His place "in the air," the Creator of the universe punches a hole through space and time, supernaturally suspending and overruling His laws of nature. His miraculous power transforms the bodies of those who have died in Him since His first coming, and they are "changed."[29] Corpses come bursting out of graves all over the planet. Funeral services are interrupted. Death is defeated and humanity's last enemy is destroyed by this Revelation Christ's resurrecting power. Hallelujah! Bodies, having been decayed and decomposed, will be mysteriously recreated. Millions of human remains, long since deteriorated in the grave, will be transformed into bodies suitable for the supernatural, freshly formatted for eternity's environment.

God designed our physical bodies to function in a physical world. But Paul says our new bodies will be "heavenly…imperishable…spiritual…not of flesh and blood…immortal…unable to die."[30] Like Jesus's resurrection body, this new kind of body will retain some familiarity from the previous life, but will also be able to do unimaginable things.[31]

So the spirits of believers who've been in heaven will be reunited with their newly resurrected bodies. Immediately following this, Christ's followers who are alive on earth at His appearance will be "caught up" together with those remade bodies to "meet the Lord in the air."

Paul, always careful and precise with his words, is moved by the Holy Spirit to choose a form of the Greek verb *harpazo* to describe this happening. This unique verb means to "seize, capture, carry off by force, claim for oneself or suddenly snatch away."[32] The Holy Spirit selected this same word to describe Philip being "snatched away" and instantly transported miles from his previous location.[33] It's also used to describe Paul's being "caught up" to heaven[34] and Jesus being "caught up" at His ascension.[35] Fourteen times this verb is used in the New Testament, and each time it refers to something or someone being seized or snatched away.[36] In five of those fourteen times, the word means to "disappear" or be "caught up to heaven."

In 1 Thessalonians 4:17, *harpazoi* is used to portray this event we call the Rapture. But two verses earlier, Paul gives it his own name, referring to it simply as the "coming of the Lord." In doing so, he uses the word *parousia,* which means "presence" or "arrival." This was a word used in ancient secular literature to announce the arrival of a king. Paul penned this word again in 2 Thessalonians 2:1, speaking of the "coming of our Lord Jesus Christ and our gathering together to Him."

Of the twenty-four times *parousia* appears in the New Testament, seventeen of these appearances refer to the future return of Jesus. Like all words in both the Old and New Testament, an individual word's nuance and meaning is determined by its grammatical form and the context in which it is found. Some of these usages of *parousia* are associated with the Rapture while other times it clearly refers to the Second Coming of Revelation 19.[37]

What an exciting word!

This *parousia* is, according to Scripture, *sudden.* But how sudden is it? How quickly does it happen? Paul tells us that it will occur "in a flash, in the twinkling of an eye."[38] As quick as lightning. Even faster.

The *parousia* event will happen so fast it will be virtually instantaneous. Before a person realizes it's occurred, it's already happened! That's how quickly we will be "caught up" and "changed." That blows my mind. What an amazing God!

And where is the evidence that the early church believed this "arrival" could happen at any time? How do we know it was prevalent throughout the worldwide community of faith in the first century?

Part of accurate Bible interpretation is getting into the minds of the original hearers and readers of Scripture. We ask ourselves, "What did Scripture's authors intend their readers to understand?" So put yourself in the skin of a first-century disciple for a moment. There's a certain simplicity they embraced that we tend to complicate and overlook.

Their Messiah had been killed.

But then He rises from the grave, defeating death and confirming His payment for sin.

He goes back to heaven after forty days of teaching.

But before doing so, He promises to return for them and take them to heaven.

The first-century disciples were very motivated by this promise. The next generation of Christians was not privileged to witness the presence and miracles of Jesus like the original disciples had. Therefore, they eagerly awaited the day of His return when they would see Him face-to-face. And they believed it could happen at any time.

This is what theologians call *imminence*, meaning it is "pending, inevitable, about to happen, forthcoming, certain to happen, next to occur." This spirit of expectancy is evident in the following verses:

- Romans 13:11—"knowing the *time*, that it is *already* the hour."[39]

- Romans 13:12—"the night is almost gone, and the day is *near*."

- 1 Corinthians 1:7—"*awaiting eagerly* the revelation of our Lord Jesus Christ."

- 1 Corinthians 16:22—"*Maranatha*" (used by the early church for "hello" or "goodbye," from an Aramaic expression meaning, "our Lord, come").

- Philippians 3:20—"for our citizenship is in heaven, from which also we *eagerly wait* for a Savior."

- Philippians 4:5—"the Lord is *near.*"

- 1 Thessalonians 1:10—"to *wait* for His Son from heaven."

- Titus 2:13—"*looking for the blessed hope* and the *appearing* of the glory of our great God and Savior, Christ Jesus."

- James 5:7,8—"Therefore be patient, brethren, until the *coming of the Lord*...be patient; strengthen your hearts, for the coming of the Lord is *near.*"

- Hebrews 9:28—"so Christ also...will *appear a second time* for salvation without reference to sin, *to those who eagerly await Him.*"

- Hebrews 10:25—"encouraging one another; and all the more *as you see the day drawing near.*"

- Hebrews 10:37—"For yet *in a very little while*, He who is coming *will come*, and will *not delay.*"

- 1 Peter 1:13—"*fix your hope* completely on the grace to be brought to you at the revelation of Jesus Christ."

- 1 Peter 4:7—"The end of all things is *near.*"

- 1 John 2:18—"we *know* that it is the *last hour.*"

- Jude 21—"*waiting anxiously* for the mercy of our Lord Jesus Christ."

- Revelation 3:11—"*I am coming quickly*; hold fast what you have."

- Revelation 22:7—"Behold, *I am coming quickly.*"
- Revelation 22:12—"Behold, *I am coming quickly.*"
- Revelation 22:20—"Yes, *I am coming quickly.*"

It's clear that Jesus's Second Coming will occur at the conclusion of the seven-year Tribulation. But if there is no *pre*tribulational *parousia* (appearance), this means the Rapture and the Second Coming are the same event, in which case there is no imminence or sense that His return can happen at any time. However, Scripture clearly documents this spirit of expectation saturating the early church, and thus the two events must be separate.

Paul further says, only those who are "in Christ" will participate in the Rapture. At a wedding, the groom is interested only in the bride. Only she is privileged to marry him. She alone captivates his attention, receives his affection, and the pledge of his faithful presence for as long as they both shall live.

The bride of Christ includes *all* believers—young and old, from every tribe, tongue, and nation throughout the church age.[40] Breaking the bonds of this earth and defying gravity's laws, they will soar heavenward, racing up toward the One who purchased them with a great price.

Only God could orchestrate such a spectacular, supernatural event.

There's nothing like it in history. Nothing so sensational, wondrous...and unexpected.

And that's exactly why this event has been preached and portrayed so dramatically. You can mock or dismiss the Rapture, but you cannot deny that when it occurs, it will send the world into mass panic and chaos.

However, for believers, it will be just the opposite experience. There will be peace instead of panic. Transformation instead of terror. Celebration, not confusion. Those Christians who are caught up will meet Jesus face-to-face, the mere thought of which brings us rapturous joy. There will be a reunion in the sky with those who have died in Christ. Imagine seeing once again someone you love who has died. Envision the explosion of emotion that moment will evoke. More joyous than a last second, game-winning touchdown or half-court buzzer-beater shot. More emotional than a soldier returning home from war. This reunion trumps all earthly home-comings, as together all Christians go to heaven!

Then, something happens that has been on the heart of Jesus since before the foundation of the world.[41] At last, His purpose in choosing us is fulfilled.

We get to be with Him.

That's what He's been longing for these two thousand years.[42] Having waited and prepared, His joy at this Rapture will be even greater than ours. Did you have any idea He loved you this much? And thus we will *always be with the Lord.*

Don't you want to be a part of Jesus's precious bride?

The Rapture goes way beyond the sensationalism of an apocalyptic movie. And it was never intended to be a salvation scare tactic. Instead, it's a *romance.* An ancient promise fulfilled. A moment in time when the bride of the ages finally beholds her bridegroom. It's when Christians realize how imperfect their vision of Jesus has been. They realize how little they thought of Him and how weak their worship of Him was. He is more majestic than the preacher had described. More powerful than He had been portrayed in books. More beautiful than they had imagined.

It is in this moment they fully realize why Paul wrote, "that at the name of Jesus every knee will bow...and every tongue will confess that Jesus Christ is Lord."[43]

This visualization helps us scratch the surface of John's words, "Beloved, now we are children of God, and it has not appeared as yet what we will be. We know that when He appears, we will be like Him, because we will see Him just as He is. And everyone who has this hope fixed on Him purifies himself, just as He is pure."[44]

Were John and Paul sensationalists? Just two more tabloid theologians? Or were they attempting to keep the church from slumbering and to get her ready for her bridegroom?

I fear today we've lost that spirit of expectation for Jesus's return. We rarely talk about it for fear of being perceived as end-times fanatics. And yet, God wants us to eagerly await the return of His Son. The Rapture is meant to infuse hope into all believers, not to be debated or dismissed. The reality of Jesus's return wasn't intended to be controversial but rather comforting. Satan would love nothing more than to turn our Lord's amazing promise into mere mockery, a modern-day joke. As Peter accurately predicted, "in the last days mockers will come with their mocking...saying, 'Where is the promise of His coming?'" (2 Peter 3:3-4).

Some today don't believe this Rapture is real. In spite of all the biblical evidence to the contrary, they still dismiss it as an overly dramatic, "recent" phenomenon. More a "wish" than a promise. But remember, Christians can disagree on interpretations of doctrines unrelated to the person of Christ or salvation. And we can also hold different views on eschatology (the study of the end times). Though I am thoroughly convinced of its certainty, believing in the Rapture is *not* essential for salvation. Even so, all Jesus's promises will be fulfilled, regardless of whether one believes in the Rapture or not. However, even in disagreement, we can still fervently love and encourage one another.

The most important thing *you* can do is to carefully examine for yourself what the Scriptures say about future events and come to a reasonable conclusion based on your study. To have *no* belief about future things is to be naïve and irresponsible. Jesus wants every one of His followers to be equipped and informed about what He's written concerning prophecy and the last days.[45] Failure to do this not only leaves us open to foolish speculation, false teaching, and misinterpretation, but it also puts our very faith on shaky ground.[46]

It's healthy to have strong beliefs, especially after careful study of the Scriptures. Believing in the Rapture doesn't make you infallible, and it shouldn't make you arrogant. It just means you're humbly confident in your belief, and secure even when someone disagrees or ridicules you.

Yes, history is building to a climactic crescendo. And while we eagerly await the sound of His voice, let us remain alert and awake! There are no prophetic signs appearing before the Rapture. So instead of looking for signs, bride, listen for His voice and look for the Lord Himself!

Are you ready?

6

Gold, Silver, and Bronze

Come with me for the next few minutes into the future. *Your* future. The date is as yet unknown. The occasion—a ceremony known as the *bema*, or the judgment seat of Christ. The purpose—to evaluate Christians' works and to give heavenly rewards to those who've spent their lives establishing and expanding God's kingdom.

In that vast heavenly arena are gathered tens of millions from every corner of the globe and every page in history. One by one, they're called to stand before the glorified Christ. Instead of a giant theater screen and highlight reel depicting the best parts of believers' lives, the supernatural omniscience of Jesus reveals the deeds done while in the flesh. Every life and ministry is carefully reviewed by the Lamb of God. Every deed and motive is tried and tested by the refining fire of His judgment. Every Christian's life is individually put through the fire, scrutinized and judged according to God's righteous expectations.

With rapt attentiveness, you hear Christ's voice echo across the great arena as He praises His choice servants. Periodically you hear Him say, "Well done, good and faithful servant," followed by a deafening roar of applause and cheers from the huge throng gathered there.

Then your name is called, and an angel escorts you to a throne where the King of kings Himself is seated. Your eyes meet and your review begins.

While I'm not exactly sure that's *how* it will happen, I am certain that it *will* happen. Paul describes it this way: "For we must all appear before the judgment seat of Christ, so that each one may be recompensed for his deeds in the body, according to what he has done, whether good or bad."[1]

So what do you think Jesus will say to you on that day? How will He respond to your life and work for Him? Perhaps a better question is, what do you *want* Him to say to you?

In that future scenario, your race is officially over. Your time on earth has come to an end. Now you stand before the Judge of the games to see what your life was really worth. To reveal what you did that *actually mattered*.

So what can we discover from Paul's words?

*First, this judgment is for **all** believers.* Paul had earlier written that "each man's work will become evident" and that "each man's praise will come to him from God."[2] Therefore, not one follower of Jesus will miss this event. Every Christian, from Pentecost to *parousia* will individually appear before this heavenly review.

*Second, it is a time of **judgment**.* Our postmodern, politically correct culture has perverted many biblical truths, redefining and misapplying them. Perhaps nowhere is that more obvious than with the word *judge*. Judging today carries one primary meaning—to condemn. To merely disagree with another person's viewpoint, morality, or lifestyle is often construed as evil and self-righteous, evoking a quick "judge not lest you be judged" response from the offended party. Ironically, those who do so commit the same perceived error in judging the ones they claim are judging them. This is unfortunate and unfair. Self-righteousness is wrong, and Jesus condemned (judged) those who committed such sin.[3] But biblical judgment goes beyond condemnation or passing sentence on someone.[4]

Specifically here, the word *bema* ("judgment seat") refers to a raised platform used in ancient athletic games.[5] At the conclusion of a race, participants were called to gather before the bema in order to receive the awards they had earned for competing in the games. Paul is using this familiar mental picture to point toward a greater reality concerning believers. As "Judge of the Games," Jesus will reward deserving participants based on a fair, just, and accurate evaluation of their lives. And this review will happen immediately following the Rapture.[6]

*Third, it's the judgment seat of **Christ**,* as the Father has given all judgment to the Son.[7]

Fourth, the basis of these rewards is "for deeds done in the body, according to what he has done, whether good or bad." This heavenly evaluation is based on what we did while living in our earthly bodies. Paul describes these deeds as "good or bad." It's important to understand a critical point here. The purpose of Christ's evaluation is *not* to determine destiny—heaven or hell. Sin is not the issue here. Our salvation is a gift from God, solely by "grace through faith, not of works."[8] There is nothing we can do for God, either before or after our salvation, that has any bearing whatsoever on our righteous standing before Him. Your forgiveness was forever settled when you trusted in Jesus's payment for sin at the cross.[9] Your salvation was sealed in Him and He declared you eternally righteous before Him. As a result, there is not an ounce of wrath or a drop of anger waiting for you in heaven. Not one sin will be brought up at the bema. To do so, Jesus would have to deny the efficacy of His own death and resurrection, not to mention contradicting His word and character. Salvation is complete. You are guilt-free.

Jesus paid it all.[10]

Instead, the purpose of the bema is to evaluate and reward us for what we did for Him after salvation. "Bad" here doesn't refer to evil or sinful acts, but is a Greek word meaning "worthless" or "not deserving recognition or reward." As Christians, it's unprofitable to waste our energy, finances, and time investing in worthless deeds and pursuits.

*Fifth, every Christian deed, along with the **motives** behind them, will be reviewed.* Paul also writes,

> Now if any man builds on the foundation with gold, sil-
> ver, precious stones, wood, hay, straw, each man's work
> will become evident; for the day will show it because it
> is to be revealed with fire, and the fire itself will test the
> quality of each man's work. If any man's work which he
> has built on it remains, he will receive a reward. If any
> man's work is burned up, he will suffer loss; but he him-
> self will be saved, yet so as through fire.[11]

The imagery here demonstrates Christ's desire to reveal those worthy deeds you did for Him. Fire quickly consumes worthless materials like wood, hay, and straw, but it has an opposite effect on precious metals. When exposed to intense heat, impurities are removed from these elements, leaving behind 100 percent pure, precious metal. In this way, Christ's evaluation will test the *quality* of our work. Notice Paul said nothing about the *quantity* of our deeds. Jesus is more concerned that we focus on the integrity of our work for Him.

This fiery judgment from Jesus, perhaps alluding to His omni-scient eyes of flaming fire we saw in chapter 3, sees past the fake and the façade. His penetrating gaze will "bring to light the things hidden in the darkness and disclose the motives of men's hearts."[12] Reviewing our Christian lives, He will torch everything we've done in His name, leaving behind only those deeds worthy of reward.

The bema evaluates deeds and motives, going beyond the *what* to the *why*. It's more than serving. It's why you served. Was it for the good feeling you got about yourself or was it for His glory? It's not just that you went on a short-term missions trip to Africa or Haiti. It's what was in your heart when you were there. Was it so you could post selfies with third-world children on Facebook and Instagram? Or was it to serve Christ and His kingdom? Did you give to your church for the tax write-off, or was your primary motive an act of worship toward God?

Yes, every deed will be evaluated. Years and years of service will be itemized, one by one. Christ's all-knowing judgment will peel back the layers, revealing what was really in our hearts in those moments we served Him. Not a single motivation will escape Him. The thoughts, desires, and emotions that drove our service to Jesus and His church will be laid bare before Him to be tested with fire.

Part of what makes this seem so intimidating is that many Christians don't think that much about their service. Therefore, the bema is a reminder to consciously dedicate every godly act to Jesus Christ and His eternal fame. But it also makes us question our own hearts. It's hard to know if every single thing we do for Christ is 100 percent *self*-free, right? Even Paul himself couldn't be sure of his motives in every situation. And even though he wasn't aware of impure motives, his conclusion was not to obsess over it but to entrust himself to God, the "one who examines me."[13] He was confident God would judge him fairly.[14] So serve with pure motives, knowing those motives will be reviewed (Romans 14:10-12).

This is exactly why Paul encouraged us to "run in such a way that you may win."[15] How we live really counts for eternity!

Unfortunately, some receive their reward here on earth. Those who work for man's praise may receive their reward in this lifetime, only to receive nothing from Christ in the next (Matthew 6:1-2,5,16). We should never assume because people praised us here that Jesus will do the same there. Again, it's what's in the heart that makes the difference.

So the bema is not just important; it's the point of your life. It's the Hall of Fame, the Academy Awards, the National Championship, the Grammys, the Super Bowl, the World Series, and the Masters all rolled into one. It's why we do what we do. And knowing who will reward us is what determines our motivation and desire to win.

"And the Award Goes to..."

In my many trips to England, I've often visited the Tower of London, located on the banks of the Thames River. Housed within that medieval fortress is Britain's Royal Collection, at the heart of which are the crown jewels, more specifically, the regalia—objects associated with the coronation of the British monarchy. Among these items are royal scepters, orbs, rings, swords, spurs, bracelets, robes, and, of course, the gem-encrusted crowns that once adorned the heads of England's kings, queens, and princes dating back to the fourteenth century. One such crown is decorated with some three thousand gems and precious stones!

The Bible says God will award crowns to deserving Christ followers. However, these crowns are a different kind of headpiece altogether. They're not the crowns of rulers but of victors. Not earthly crowns but heavenly ones. Not perishable but imperishable and unfading. Not given to kings but given by a King. The New Testament word is *stephanos*, or wreath, referring to intertwined olive branches bestowed at the Greek national games. These bema crowns are awarded to those who excel in a particular category of life.[16]

So if God promises crowns to certain of His servants, what exactly are they, and how does He decide who gets them? Scripture lists five specific crowns awarded to those whose service merits them.

1. The Imperishable Crown (1 Corinthians 9:24-27)—Given to those who exercise self-control as they run the race of service set before them. These individuals are focused, remaining true to their life purpose. They refuse anything that denies them the prize or holds them back, disciplining their body for the sake of godliness. They run the race well, staying in their lane and sprinting all the way to the finish line.

2. The Crown of Righteousness (2 Timothy 4:6-8)—Awarded to those who look toward and love the appearing of Jesus. Their lives are blameless before Him, so much so that when He suddenly appears, they are not ashamed.

3. The Crown of Life (James 1:12; Revelation 2:10)—Awarded to those who persevere under trials and persecution, and who are faithful to Jesus until death.

4. The Crown of Exultation/Rejoicing (1 Thessalonians 2:19-20)—Awarded to those who win others to Christ.

5. The Crown of Glory (1 Peter 5:1-4)—Awarded to obedient pastors/elders who faithfully shepherd the flock of God.

These are brief descriptions since the Bible doesn't explain or describe them in greater detail. This could be because Jesus prefers that we focus on pursuing what precipitates these crowns—discipline, purpose, expectancy, holiness, purity, perseverance, being a witness, and faithfulness—rather than chasing the crowns themselves. When we focus on serving Christ, He will give us what we deserve.

But is that all? Will Jesus give any other kind of reward in heaven? I believe the answer is yes. Though we don't know the full extent of how Christ will reward His bride at the bema, there are several truths Scripture affirms for us.

God's Word states that whoever encourages, supports, and ministers to those receiving rewards in heaven will also share in their reward. Jesus said, "He who receives a prophet in the name of a prophet shall receive a prophet's reward; and he who receives a righteous man in the name of a righteous man shall receive a righteous man's reward."[17] So if you helped someone run their race well, you will share in their reward.

But there appear to be additional ways Christ will reward His followers at the bema. Jesus also considered acts of compassion or kindness done toward His children to be done to Him as well.[18] Such acts will not go unnoticed or unrewarded.[19]

Though not specifically referring to the bema, Jesus indicates greater authority and responsibility will be given to those who are faithful stewards of what God has given them. [20] According to Matthew 20:17-28, Jesus says greatness in God's future kingdom is directly proportionate to how we serve others right now. There will also be verbal praise from Jesus as well, as Paul writes in 1 Corinthians 4:5, "then each man's praise will come to him from God." He even disciplines us when we are disobedient, training us in righteousness with a view to potential reward. [21]

God is deeply committed to making us more like Jesus, from the moment we come to faith to the moment we stand before His Son. [22] This is evidence that all true believers will do *something* worthwhile for Christ.

Another heavenly reward may be an increased ability to praise or proclaim God's glory in eternity. Daniel 12:3 seems to indicate this as those who influence others toward righteousness will "shine brightly like the brightness of the expanse of heaven…like the stars forever and ever."

Though some things about future rewards may be unclear, of this we can be sure. Serve Christ now and He will reward you later.

That's His promise to you.

Crown Me with Many Crowns

Once, while speaking on stewardship at a couples' retreat, I mentioned how badly I wanted to receive rewards from Christ at the bema. Afterward, a man rebuked me for my "selfish approach to serving God." I explained (gracefully, I hope) that if he had listened to the last part of my message, he would have heard my motivation for wanting those rewards. And just for the record, I unapologetically confess that I still desperately want to receive rewards from Jesus at the bema.

But it's a fair question. Is there anything selfish about this desire to receive heavenly rewards? I suppose it could be, if we fail to understand the true nature of the rewards (and crowns) Jesus will give.

We gain that understanding through a sneak preview God gives us regarding these heavenly crowns. In Revelation 4:9-11 we read,

> And when the living creatures give glory and honor and thanks to Him who sits on the throne, to Him who lives forever and ever, the twenty-four elders will fall down before Him who sits on the throne, and will worship Him who lives forever and ever, and will cast their crowns before the throne, saying,
>
>> "Worthy are You, our Lord and our God, to receive glory and honor and power; for You created all things, and because of Your will they existed, and were created."

I believe the twenty-four elders here represent redeemed humanity (the bride) from the church age.[23] They fit the biblical description of the bride elsewhere, clothed in "white garments," picturing their righteousness in Christ.[24] And they haven't come to God's throne empty-handed since part of their worship includes casting their golden crowns before the throne.

But why? Why would you remove the crown you just received? Why lay down the heavenly reward you spent your entire Christian life earning? There's only one reason, revealed in verse 11. Something happens to the bride when she arrives in heaven, something she caught only glimpses of while on earth. Once there, she becomes fully convinced of a truth she had previously heard. At last, three words come bursting forth from her heart, washing over her soul in a tidal wave of worship.

He is worthy.

She can say those words now. Previously read in a Bible or a book or sung with teary eyes and hands lifted high, now they have become real. Until that day when she falls down before Him who sits on the heavenly throne, she will never completely absorb the full meaning of those three words. Paul alluded to this experience when he said, "For now we see in a mirror dimly, but then face to face; now I know in part, but then I will know fully just as I also have been fully known."[25]

In that glorious moment, we'll finally experience what the cherubim and seraphim have known for ages. There, with our faces bowed before heaven's throne, we will finally get it. We will grasp the magnitude of His inestimable worth as God. Words like *glory, worthy,* and *praise,* often tritely spoken while on earth, will take on new dimensions in that day. Our crowned heads will comprehend why our God rightfully deserves "glory, honor, and power."

In Revelation 4:11, John lists two primary reasons why Jesus is worthy.

1. He is the Creator of all things. Everything that *is* owes its existence to Him. Space. Planets. Solar systems. Clusters. Millions of galaxies. Billions of stars. Billions of light-years separating each of them. Superclusters. The universe. Earth. Mankind. You. Molecules. Atoms. Quarks. Gluons, electrons, and neutrinos. He made them all. How utterly foolish that one of God's creations, with finite intelligence, could be so arrogant as to propose another explanation for our existence. If it weren't so sinful and stupid, it would actually be comical.

2. All things exist and were created because of His will. Being in His presence catapults the bride into realizing that God made all that there is simply because He wanted to. It pleased Him to do so. And therefore everything that exists not only is created *by* Him but *for* Him (Colossians 1:16).

You and I will cast our crowns because we realize we exist not so we could merely enjoy life, but so that we could enjoy *Christ.* To find in Him our ultimate purpose and reason to live is the pinnacle of human discovery. How would our lives change if we could experience a greater realization of that truth right now?

Of course I want to have a crown to cast at His feet! Because it all circles back to the one who is worthy. More heavenly rewards mean a greater capacity to worship with satisfaction and joy, not regret. It means we can offer a greater sacrifice of praise, honoring Him who sits on the throne.

Some say we shouldn't pray for God's favor on our lives. But why not? More favor now means more worship then. We ought to pray, *Lord, bless me so I can serve Your kingdom's cause and bless You back with praise in heaven.*

Crowns and rewards are not bestowed so we can proclaim how great we are, because we know who's really behind any good thing or success we experience down here.[26] If receiving rewards and crowns means we can bring greater praise to Him, then we'd be fools not to work toward earning them because it's all about *Him*!

Now you know why these crowned saints are so filled with praise and motivated to remove their crowns and place them before His throne. They are so moved to fall down and worship because He is worthy. This praise is an appropriate gift for a King who is worthy to receive honor because He is honorable, worthy to receive power because He is powerful, worthy for all creation to praise Him because He created all things, even worthy enough for all created things to find their ultimate purpose and meaning in Him because He created them for His pleasure and for His perfect plan. And so heaven worships God simply because He deserves it.

"Your Attention, Please"

Try to imagine the sheer number of redeemed humanity that will one day gather in heaven. Billions. Perhaps more. A sea of worshippers. A mega-mass of rescued sinners as well as angelic beings. As far as the eye can see. There appears to be no end to them. Can you see it?

John tells us this huge multitude begins to shout, and they're all declaring the same thing. Together. With one voice, there is incredible unity in heaven as these countless souls burst into a chorus of praise.

> Then I looked, and I heard the voice of many angels around the throne and the living creatures and the elders; and the number of them was myriads of myriads, and thousands of thousands, saying with a loud voice,
>
> > "Worthy is the Lamb that was slain to receive power and riches and wisdom and might and honor and glory and blessing."
>
> And every created thing which is in heaven and on the earth and under the earth and on the sea, and all things in them, I heard saying,
>
> > "To Him who sits on the throne, and to the Lamb, be blessing and honor and glory and dominion forever and ever."
>
> And the four living creatures kept saying, "Amen." And the elders fell down and worshiped. [27]

All of heaven's attention focuses on the Lamb of God, the Lord Jesus Christ. He is the centerpiece of heaven, the intersection of every syllable of praise. He is:

- Worthy to be praised because He was slain.
- Worthy to be the recipient of all power, riches, wisdom, might, honor, glory, and blessing.
- Worthy enough for us to submit our will to Him and to relinquish ownership of all our possessions. Everything we have is His. Is He that worthy? Heaven seems to think so.

Joining this celestial praise festival is "every created thing" (v. 13). Even those spirits in hell must recognize the greatness and glory of the One who is the Alpha and Omega. In the midst of their torment, their minds are still lucid. They know the truth now better than at any time on earth. They know exactly who Jesus is, and they are compelled by His worth to declare His Lordship on bended knee. [28] Wow!

Could this God be so great that literally every living thing shouts praise to Him? How wonderful must He be to deserve this kind of honor? A sense of awe fills our hearts when thinking of a truth like this. While we hang out down here, up in heaven they're exalting a God who is worthy!

To that we can only say with the angels, "Amen," which means, "yes, I agree" or "may it be so." And the elders fell down and worshipped. And so do we.

So What Now?

How can we possibly respond to such potent truth about the bema and our heavenly worship? How does that future reality influence our present experience? Let's look at three words that help us nail down a solid game plan and life perspective in light of God's Awards Day.

Fear

After speaking of the bema, Paul concludes, "Therefore, knowing the *fear* of the Lord, we persuade men." [29]

Wait. Fear? I thought fear was the last thing we should experience as believers. Didn't all our fear leave when we trusted Christ? Isn't "fear not" the most often repeated command in the Bible, occurring nearly 150 times? Didn't Paul say that God "gave us a spirit not of fear"? [30] Didn't John write, "There is no fear in love, but perfect love casts out fear"? [31]

The answer to all those questions is yes.

In 2 Corinthians 5, however, Paul is talking about the bema, stating that fear should motivate us toward serving Christ. So how do we explain this?

First, fear in its unhealthy, toxic form births anxiety, which leads toward panic or an emotional spiral into depression. That's not the fear Paul is referring to here. *Fear* in this context means a "reverential awe" or a "worshipful respect." It means considering who it is you're serving and how deserving He is of your allegiance and service, and then living in light of that deep respect. Paul cited this kind of fear as motivation for us to pursue a lifestyle of holiness.[32] It's the same fear that kept the early believers at peace and built up the church.[33] It's the fear Solomon spoke of that imparts wisdom and a clear perspective on life.[34]

When considering how great our God is, and Revelation's vision of His regal glory and infinite worth, we are naturally captivated with awe. As a result, bringing honor to this God becomes our greatest passion and pursuit. Seeing who Jesus really is produces wonder, admiration, respect, amazement, astonishment, reverence, esteem, and worship. And the practical "so what" of that filters down into our everyday lives in tangible ways.

Second, this healthy fear is not phobic, causing us to cower in fright. Rather, it causes us to contemplate the possibility of not receiving the Lord's pleasure and approval at the bema. In a proper way, we're concerned about loss of rewards. We fear leading a mediocre life, wasting our time on things that don't matter. We fear living a life that fails to achieve its greatest potential.

One of my seminary professors, Dr. Howard Hendricks, used to regularly remind us, "Gentlemen, fear not that your lives shall come to an end. Rather, fear that they may never have a beginning."

Not experiencing a full life of service to Christ leads to regret, not reward.

Third, Paul says this "fear of the Lord" motivates us to "persuade men." The apostle was concerned the Corinthians might embrace false teaching over the godly instruction he'd given them. Should this happen, they would lose heavenly reward at the bema.[35]

We see this principle in other areas of life as well. The desire to compete and win is part of what motivates great athletes to play their best. But the negative thought (fear) of losing also drives them to pursue victory. The same is true concerning the bema. Paul saw himself as a competitor, determined to win. How awesome then must our God be that when we see Him, we will either desperately wish or jubilantly celebrate that our life had been devoted to Him?

Focus

This godly fear gives us clarity, bringing our life perspective into focus.

Apart from those competing in the decathlon, most Olympic athletes specialize in one field of competition. Boxers don't run the 100-meter dash and pole-vaulters don't compete in the shot put. Rather, each athlete narrows their field of competition to one thing. All of their training is designed to contribute toward their main goal—Win Gold. Predawn workouts. Regimented diets. Limited social contact. Rearranged priorities. Strength training. Workouts. More workouts. Competitive races. These world-class athletes put everything aside for their dreams of Olympic glory. They often relocate for months at a time in order to clear their minds, enabling them to concentrate on their one goal. There's no time to waste time. Too much is at stake. They're willing to do whatever it takes to achieve their highest purpose as an athlete. Everything else is secondary.

Because of Paul's desire to bring honor to Christ and be rewarded at the bema, he narrowed his life purpose to "know nothing among you but Jesus Christ, and Him crucified."[36] In 1 Corinthians 9, his mindset paralleled that of an Olympian. And what did this focus look like in his life as a result?

- Doing whatever it took to achieve his goal of reaching others (v. 22)

- Promoting and partaking of the gospel as his life objective (v. 23)

- Not being content to run unless he was running to win (v. 24)

- Exercising self-control to keep his mind and lifestyle on track (v. 25)

- Refusing to waste time and energy on peripheral priorities and pursuits, targeting instead specific goals (v. 26)

- Disciplining his body, preventing its urges from controlling him and disqualifying him from the race (v. 27)

How ironic that many of us receive education and training for a job, spending tens of thousands of dollars in the process, but when it comes to training for our primary mission in life, we often wing it. And we wonder why we're consistently defeated by sin and fail to regularly experience God's power in living. It's because the race is long and difficult. Our spiritual muscles are underdeveloped and weak, so we give in to temptation and are emotionally crushed when life hits us with difficult circumstances. And our effectiveness for God's kingdom is minimalized.

But it doesn't have to be this way. These Scriptures help us become focused by asking ourselves:

- What am I really building my life on? Temporal or eternal things? Physical or spiritual? Worthless or valuable? Trivial or significant? Am I gathering straw or mining silver? Whatever it is, the fire will reveal it.

- Am I running in the right race? Is my life centered on Christ or some other primary pursuit?

- Am I helping others win?

- Am I running to win or merely showing up, casually meandering through the race?

- Am I running with the right motives? Who am I seeking to please? Whose applause and approval do I seek? Whose glory am I promoting? Is it about Him or secretly all about me? Is the ministry I am serving in an ego-booster or a Jesus-promoter? Am I using service to prop up my weak self-esteem or to lift up and spread His fame? Do I care who gets the credit and recognition? Do I serve for earthly gain or to store up a spiritual savings account in heaven?

- Am I even serving Him at all?

Granted, our hearts can be deceptive and we can't always fully know our motives.[37] But we *can* take a gut check on our hearts and minds from time to time. As someone who has been in full-time vocational ministry for over thirty years, I've had to ask myself many times, *Jeff, why do you serve Christ? What if there were no recognition or reward in this life, no public acknowledgment of your service? Would you still do it? Is He worth it?*

Faithfulness

The third and final word helping us respond to the reality of the bema is *faithfulness*. I'm thankful that God doesn't require perfection, because I'd be in big trouble. Instead, He only wants faithfulness.[38] Just take the one day the Father has given you and max out on faithfulness. Do what you can do and do it well. And pay attention to the small things.

Inconsistency is a plague we must avoid. Many Christians today inconsistently gather with fellow believers on Sundays and rarely engage God's Word on their own. This must change. God is looking for people He can count on. Can He count on you? Faithfulness doesn't mean you never fail. It means you get up after you fall and continue in the race. One day at a time. All the way to the finish line.

Can You Hear?

I played baseball throughout my childhood. When I was twelve, the Dixie Youth League played its games at a neighborhood park in my hometown of Anderson, South Carolina. Embler Field was a slice of old-school Americana. The outfield wall and dugouts were painted cinderblock. The press box sat above the snow-cone stand behind home plate. And old wooden bleachers gave friends, fans, and families a place to cheer from. There were no digital scoreboards, just a kid with a big piece of chalk. I can still recall the feel of cotton uniforms and the summer smell of sweat and Double Bubble bubblegum.

But there was this one kid on my team who was different. Randy was the first deaf person I'd ever met. He wore a hearing aid, and I'd never seen a hearing aid on anyone under seventy. Due to his condition, Randy spoke with a distinct and *loud* voice, and us guys didn't quite know how to relate to him. Occasionally, a teammate would snicker at him or poke fun at the way he spoke. But Randy didn't care. He just wanted to play baseball.

Our practices were in the afternoons, and each time when we were done, Coach Johnson would call us in to talk about the next practice or upcoming game. Sprinting in from right field, Randy would race to the huddle around the pitcher's mound. And while the rest of us were thinking about going home and getting supper, Randy would burst through his teammates, run straight up to our coach, and with wide-eyed enthusiasm, he'd ask, "Did I do good, Mr. Johnson? Did I do good?"

This happened after *every* practice.

I'll admit that, as a twelve-year-old, that became a bit irritating. However, it wasn't until many years later that I understood Randy's true motive. He didn't care that his hat was off-kilter or that his glove was an off brand. He wasn't really concerned about what the rest of us guys thought. The only thing that mattered to that young boy was simply that he had pleased his coach. He practiced and played for one man's approval. *His* praise was what Randy sweat for. And no practice was too grueling, no effort too great just as long as Coach Johnson endorsed his efforts.

And the man clearly understood it. At every single practice, Coach Johnson would break into a compassionate smile and rest his hand on Randy's sweaty ball-capped head. He'd jostle it around a bit and say, "You did great, Randy. I'm proud of you. Good job, son."

I encourage you to regularly take time just to listen. Get apart from the polluting noise of your everyday life and listen forward. Pay close attention to the voice of your future. Lean in and tune in to the sound of your eternity. Can you hear the multitude in heaven cheering you on?

Can you feel the deafening roar of the stadium?

Can you see them on their feet?

Can you hear their life examples shouting to you, "It's worth it. *He's* worth it! Live for Christ. Invest in eternity. Run the race. Don't quit!"

And can you envision the Worthy One smiling and saying to you, "Well done, good and faithful servant. You did great, My child. I am so proud of you!"

That moment will make all your sacrifice, suffering, and perseverance dissolve into insignificance. Paul put it this way, "For I consider that the sufferings of this present time are not worthy to be compared with the glory that is to be revealed to us."[39] On that day, you will fully know what you now know only in part—that *nothing* you do for Christ is ever wasted.[40]

Go big for Him, my friend. Go for gold!

7

Meanwhile, in Heaven...a Throne

Imagine you're a Christian living late in the first century. Beginning around AD 67, intense persecution of the church began under the Roman emperor Nero.[1] Intoxicated by his own ego, this man is widely believed to be responsible for setting the infamous fire in Rome, which killed thousands. He subsequently blamed this disaster on Christians, thus further justifying his torture and murder of them.

One of his successors was an arrogant, cruel person named Domitian (AD 81–96). Tall in stature, he preferred to be addressed as *dominus et deus* ("master and god"). His brother Titus, serving under their emperor father, Vespasian, had in AD 70 crushed the Jewish rebellion in Jerusalem, destroying their temple. This is one reason Revelation's prophecies could not have been fulfilled in the first century as John didn't receive his vision until some twenty-five years after these events. Therefore, Revelation must point to a future time in history.[2]

However, so proud was Domitian that "he commanded himself to be worshipped as god, and that images of gold and silver in his honour should be set up in the capital."[3]

During this period of extreme persecution, believers were brought before Roman magistrates and given a "test oath" to see if their allegiance was to their emperor or to their Christ. Those who refused to take the oath were sentenced to death. If they confessed Christ, their fate was the same. And what did they have to look forward to? For admitting faith in Jesus, believers were seared with hot irons, boiled alive, burned, scourged, stoned, and hanged. Many had their bodies torn apart while others were thrown upon the horns of wild bulls. Friends of these murdered martyrs were refused the privilege of burying the remains.[4]

In addition to being murdered, early Christians were also made into objects of amusement—sewn up inside the hides of beasts and torn to death by dogs, crucified, or locked inside a brass bull and roasted alive. Others were dressed in shirts made stiff with wax, fixed to a wooden beam, and set on fire as human candles to light Nero's gardens.[5]

Early church father Justin Martyr writes, "Though beheaded, and crucified, and thrown to wild beasts, and chains, and fire, and all other kinds of torture, we do not give up our confession; but, the more such things happen, the more do others in larger numbers become faithful."[6]

To the Roman government, Christianity was a "deadly superstition."[7] Followers of Jesus were called "atheists" for not believing in Rome's gods. Christians' refusal to sacrifice to the gods was considered the equivalent of sacrilege and treason.[8] There were widespread rumors that these Christians practiced cannibalism (they ate the body of Jesus during communion), orgies (the weekly agape love-feasts), and even incest and immorality (their fervent love for brothers and sisters). To the Roman mind, Christianity sounded like paganism, providing Rome's officials and citizens plenty of ammunition to fuel their distrust and disdain for the weird cult many called "The Way."[9]

If you were a Christian living in AD 95, you were under constant threat of persecution. Believers were marginalized, misunderstood, and demonized in a culture that lauded its own morality as superior to that of Christians.

Sound familiar?

Scripture states that during the end times, a revived Roman Empire will arise as a ten-nation confederation, ultimately headed by the antichrist.[10] I believe we are seeing the spirit of that end-times empire in our world today. It is vehemently anti-Christian and anti-Semitic. Though we in America are not yet experiencing the same type of persecution the early church suffered, two things we do know.

First, hatred toward passionate followers of Jesus is steadily growing. If you doubt this, try speaking up for marriage as being only between one man and one woman. Share what the Bible teaches about homosexuality, creationism, the inerrancy of Scripture, or the exclusive claims of Jesus Christ as the only true God. Do this in a blog, on Facebook or Twitter, or among your work associates and see what wrath and ridicule the world unleashes upon you. You will likely be labeled a "mindless moron" or "bigoted bully." You may lose friends or even your job.

But as Judeo-Christian values continue to be attacked and systematically removed from society, you will have no choice but to stand before the court of public opinion and declare your allegiance for Christ alone. No, we aren't yet being killed for our faith. But we are seeing a consistent, increasing opposition to Christians and their Jesus.

Second, we in the West are often sheltered and insulated from the persecution and martyrdom of believers all across the world. As you read these words, Christians are being shot, beheaded, scourged, crucified, and burned alive in kilns. And their crime? Blasphemy against Islam. Owning a Bible. Taking communion wine.[11] They receive the death penalty just for confessing Christ as Savior and Lord.

Rome would be so proud.

And is it so far-fetched to think that one day we could experience similar persecution in America?

In a 2009 document released by the Office of Intelligence Analysis (Department of Homeland Security), certain "right-wing extremist" groups are listed as potential "threats to the government." Among these are "groups, movements and individuals" that are those opposed to abortion, and certain radicals who believe in "end times" prophecies.[12] Biblical views such as these are increasingly considered "extreme" and "anti-government." How long before Washington officially begins censoring historical Christian beliefs as "hate speech"? Already being crucified in (social) media, sued and fined for standing against homosexual marriage (even though fully embracing homosexuals with Christ's love), how long before Christ-followers are thrown in prison for their beliefs?

We are not the majority here, people. And Jesus warned us this would happen.

> "If the world hates you, you know that it has hated Me
> before it hated you. If you were of the world, the world
> would love its own; but because you are not of the world,
> but I chose you out of the world, because of this the
> world hates you. Remember the word that I said to you,
> 'A slave is not greater than his master.' If they persecuted
> Me, they will also persecute you; if they kept My word,
> they will keep yours also. But all these things they will
> do to you for My name's sake, because they do not know
> the One who sent Me."[13]

How much clearer can Christ make it? The world is not going to give you a standing ovation for following Jesus. You are not of the world and you don't belong to this world system.[14] Your allegiance is with Jesus and your citizenship is in heaven. Those inebriated with the world's values recognize you as a foreigner, and they ultimately hate you for not conforming.

However, they hated Jesus before they hated you, and for the very same reasons. They didn't hate Jesus because He was a nice, loving guy who did miracles and fed the hungry, healed the sick, and brought people back to life. They hated Him because His life, love, and words exposed their sin.[15] So they killed Him for it. Jesus says. "If you follow Me, eventually the world will get around to hating and persecuting you too. *Bank* on it, beloved."

But Scripture is equally clear that we are never to be rude, abrasive, or sinfully angry when living out our beliefs for Christ.[16] Even so, in today's climate, the slightest moral noise coming from Christians is denounced as evil. So we may have more in common with those early believers than we think.

At the close of the first century, Jesus's bride faced ambiguity about what awaited her in the days and years ahead. The Messiah had come and had revealed who God was. He fulfilled the Old Testament prophecies and inaugurated a new covenant. He became a willing substitute for sin at the cross, and then conquered death by rising from the grave. But that had been some sixty years previous. In the meantime, the church had grown through infancy and into adolescence. She had deepened her knowledge of Christ and His Word through the Gospels and letters from the apostles and had expanded His kingdom through the preaching of the gospel. Persecution had strengthened and purified her. But now, as the canon of Scripture was nearing completion, the first-century church would also need a heavy dose of hope for the future.

Additionally, because of what they would read about God's plan in the following chapters of Revelation, they also needed some supernatural reassurance. As far as they knew, Revelation's prophecies could happen at any time due to the expected and imminent return of Jesus. Hearing the full contents of Revelation, those believers would undoubtedly, like John in Revelation 1:17, have been overwhelmed by the coming catastrophic prophecies and global judgments. And just like those first-century believers, we too live in a strange, uncertain, and potentially prophetic moment in history.

The View

Jesus could have revealed John's apocalyptic vision any way He desired. However, before subjecting the apostle to the traumatic truths of end-times judgments, He shows John an open door in heaven. John hears the same loud voice he'd heard in 1:10, and the speaker diverts his attention away from earth, inviting John to "come up here, and I will show you what must take place after these things."[17] The aged apostle is immediately and supernaturally transported into heaven.

Revelation's prophecies are best understood from heaven's vantage point, which provides us with a panoramic view of things to come. What we see from this location lifts our minds above the confusing chaos and disorienting fog of earth's perspective. One of the biggest obstacles we face in wrapping our minds around the events of the Tribulation is that our thinking is often earthbound. When it comes to prophecy, our thoughts can become grounded by human insight, limiting our understanding. The gravitational pull of conventional thinking weighs us down, preventing us from experiencing the objectivity of God's camera angle. Therefore, seeing Revelation through heaven's lens is essential to getting a firm grasp on these truths. Like an eagle watching an earthquake, we see these events but are not devastated by them.

So the unique perspective from heaven is critical to John's comprehension of these future things. But that's not all. What John sees *in* heaven also becomes a game-changer in his perspective. But what does he see? What *immediately* catches his eye and captivates his attention?

A throne.

In just ten verses, John mentions "throne" or "thrones" *thirteen* times. This repetition is not only John's effort to accurately describe what he saw, but also serves to emphasize a critical point. So what does God want His church to know about this heavenly throne?

It's Occupied (4:2)

An occupied throne means God's rule is established and unmovable. It signifies that Someone is at the wheel, driving history, and that mankind is not traveling down a purposeless path. The One who occupies this throne is in charge, a fact that obliterates the foolish belief that human free will is king and that there exists no ultimate meaning in life. If this throne-occupying God truly exists, then history, humanity, and *your life* all have genuine purpose and destiny.

It's Beautiful (4:3)

John sees the One on the throne as having the appearance of "a jasper stone" and "a sardius." This jasper is later described as "crystal clear," which suggests a diamond-like appearance.[18] God is on His throne, refracting the brilliance of His glory as if through a diamond. Sardius is a ruby-red stone. Around this throne is "a rainbow" that has heavy emerald-green overtones. This encircling rainbow radiance is described by Ezekiel as "the glory of the Lord."[19]

Consider how beautiful all this must be to John. His first-century eyes can only draw upon earthly color comparisons to describe God upon His throne. This is why he describes it as "*like* a jasper...*like* an emerald." Imagine the brilliance of colors in heaven, as of yet unseen by human eyes and unimagined by mortal minds. And these are mere human words and illustrative descriptions of our great God. Can we even conceive of the reality of such a sight? No, not yet. God's throne scene is beautiful beyond words.

It's Honored (4:4)

Around this throne are "twenty-four elders." Again, these elders represent the redeemed bride of Christ, evidenced by their white garments, golden crowns, and joint rule with Christ.[20] They cannot be angels because angelic beings are nowhere described in Scripture as sitting on thrones or receiving crowns. In the New Testament, the word *elder* typically applies to church leaders.

But why the number twenty-four? Some have suggested this number represents the twelve tribes of Israel and the twelve apostles. However, Scripture implies that Old Testament saints will not be resurrected and rewarded until after the Tribulation.[21] Further, Jesus said the apostles would not receive their thrones until after His Second Coming and millennial reign.[22] This leads many to conclude these elders are a representative figure of the priestly role of New Testament believers, and that the number twenty-four is used the same way it was in 1 Chronicles 24 when David divided the tribe of Levi into twenty-four heads, representing the whole number of priests.

But the elders' presence around the throne is more than symbolism. More from these elders in a minute.

It's Righteous (4:5)

John witnesses "flashes of lightning" as a loud thunderstorm bursts from this throne. Thunder alerts us toward the sky, and whether it appears as a sudden clap or an ominous roll, it's usually a sign that a great storm is coming. All throughout the book of Revelation, we hear loud thunder.[23] John's "weather report" forecasts a righteous and wrathful God about to unleash His fury upon the earth. Seven burning lamps also burn before the throne, "which are the seven Spirits of God." The number seven is repeated fifty-four times throughout the book of Revelation, more than any other number.[24] Seven is often associated with perfection or completion,[25] and here likely symbolizes the Holy Spirit.

It's Holy (4:6-11)

Around this magnificent throne is a crystal-like sea of glass. In close proximity to it are "four living creatures." These are undoubtedly angels, specifically cherubim, and match similar descriptions of heavenly creatures witnessed by Isaiah and Ezekiel.[26] This order of angelic beings was assigned to guard the way to the tree of life after Adam and Eve were expelled from Eden.[27] A representation of them made out of gold was part of the mercy seat that covered the ark of the covenant.[28] Lucifer was from this order of angels, and is believed by some to have covered God's throne.[29]

These "living creatures" are described as being "full of eyes in front and behind," referring to their comprehensive knowledge and awareness. John sees them portrayed "like a lion...a calf...a face like a man...a flying eagle." Though obviously symbolic language, these descriptions help us understand their nature and role. A lion represents majesty and strength. A calf perhaps signifies humble service. A likeness of a man may denote intelligence or rational thought, and an eagle symbolizes great vision and speedy service in their mission for God. Ezekiel seems to suggest that all cherubs possess all four of these characteristics.[30] Each of them also has six wings. According to Isaiah, two wings cover their face, two cover their feet, and two are for flying.[31]

Wild descriptions, right? And what are they doing at the throne? Well, they're not receiving mercy as we currently do.[32] Rather, these bizarre-looking beings incessantly proclaim a core truth about the God they serve: "Holy, holy, holy is the Lord God, the Almighty, who was and who is and who is to come."

There's a perpetual refrain in heaven, just as there was in Isaiah's day.[33] And according to the ancient prophet, they're not just proclaiming praise to God but also declaring this fundamental truth to one another as well. They repeat the one attribute of God they want heaven and earth and the bride to know about Him. Of all the truths about God these supernaturally intelligent creatures could have chosen—love, grace, mercy, faithfulness, and so on—they are compelled to passionately proclaim that *He is holy*.

But why? Doesn't the Bible say God is love? And what about all

His other wonderful characteristics? Why not "Love, love, love"? The answer is simple. The cherubim know something we don't. These angels serving God in closest proximity to His throne understand something about God's *essence*, something at the heart of His nature. We're used to praising God for the things He does that relate to us. That's because, even in our faith, our flawed nature subconsciously makes us the center of our spiritual universe. It's not intentional, but a subtle selfishness often rises to the surface even in our worship. Yes, we sincerely love God. But *why*? If we dug deep enough into our hearts, we may discover that the motivation for adoring this God we serve has its roots in the benefits we get from that relationship. But this isn't a sin issue or something that's morally wrong with us. It's a natural part of our humanity and spiritual development. And as we'll see, there *are* personal benefits to understanding and encountering the nature of God.

However, our tendency is to swing the pendulum far beyond its healthy boundaries. At its worst, this kind of praise relegates God to merely a tool we use to get what we naturally crave—meaning, happiness, fulfillment, joy, friends, good feelings. Taken to the extreme, God ultimately exists for our benefit, not vice versa. Part of this is due, as already mentioned, to the fact that we're fallen beings with inherently selfish hearts. But this thinking is also fed by a consumer-driven Christian culture obsessed with marketing Jesus's benefits to the church. We do this in an effort to get the disciples' attention and perhaps rouse them from their spiritual slumber for a few minutes on Sunday. We think maybe then the church will somehow experience revival and change the world with the gospel.

But heaven is focused, not on God's benefits but on God Himself. What captivates these four creatures' attention is not just what He can do but rather who He is. These angels cry "Holy, holy, holy" not so they can get a warm feeling inside, but simply to ascribe pure praise to the One who deserves it.

When we hear the word *holiness*, we typically think of God being

morally perfect and without sin. That's true. However, this is a secondary meaning of the word. Throughout the Bible, the word translated "holy" primarily means "to be *separate* or *set apart*." [34] What the
angels are doing is more than praising God for His moral perfection. They go deeper, worshipping the God they serve because of
His transcendence above all things. God is highly exalted, set apart
from His creation. He is a "wholly other" being, unlike any other.
Isaiah records God's own words regarding Himself,

> "To whom then will you liken Me
> That I should be his equal?" says the Holy One. [35]

God desires that this truth about Him be cemented in our minds.
He is incomparable. Unequaled. Unlike any human or angel. This
attribute of God is "incommunicable," meaning we can never experience it ourselves. As finite creations, we have a beginning point in
time. God does not. We are limited in every way. God has no limits. As He previously proclaimed to Isaiah,

> "For my thoughts are not your thoughts,
> Nor are your ways My ways," declares the Lord.
> "For as the heavens are higher than the earth,
> So are My ways higher than your ways
> And My thoughts than your thoughts." [36]

And exactly how high are the heavens above the earth? "Heavens"
refers to the vast array of stars we see in the night sky. Of course we
now know there is much more out there beyond the four thousand
or so stars the human eye can see. There is a solar system beyond
them. And a galaxy beyond the solar system. Billions of stars in our
galaxy, separated by millions of light years between them. And a
universe beyond all that, containing millions of galaxies like ours.
It's outer space, and it goes on in every direction for what seems like
infinity.

Infinity. The very word causes our mind's hard drive to crash. We just can't go there mentally. It's too much. Too great. Too far. Our thoughts stretch like arms reaching up for an object on a shelf. We get on intellectual tiptoes, only to realize this truth is much farther than we can grasp.

Holiness is the sum total of all God's attributes. His love is holy. His grace is holy. His justice is holy. This fact about God is so distant, so beyond our mortal comprehension that it eventually leads us to only one logical conclusion. There's only one place a thinking mind can go after contemplating the magnitude of this brilliant, shining star of truth. Like traveling trillions of light-years into space and looking back toward Earth, we begin to grasp our smallness as human beings.

This God is not like us.

He is beyond. Infinite. Great. Separate. Different. Unrivaled. Unequaled. Without any peers. And when this realization reenters the atmosphere of our minds, crashing into our heart-soil, there is only one thing left for us to do.

Worship.

It's the only response worthy of the truth that has been revealed to us. And these galactically endowed cherubim know it. *That's* why they cry out, "Holy, holy, holy is the Lord God, the Almighty, who was and who is and who is come."[37] This Holy One is perpetually present. He has no beginning and He has no end.[38] He is Yahweh, the "I AM WHO I AM" that spoke to Moses from the burning bush.[39]

Are you worshipping yet?

The angels extol this God for who He is, giving Him what He deserves—"glory and honor and thanks." By their ongoing act of worship, the twenty-four elders prompt the rest of Jesus's bride in a glorious chorus of praise. As we previously saw, they "fall down," publicly displaying their utter humility before this enthroned, eternal God. They voluntarily remove the crowns Jesus has awarded them at the bema, casting them before the throne. So motivated is

the bride that she showers her God with gifts He Himself made possible, reminding us of Paul's words, "For from Him and through Him and to Him are all things. To Him be the glory forever. Amen."[40]
And this becomes our spoken anthem of praise,

> "Worthy are You, our Lord and our God, to receive glory and honor and power; for You created all things, and because of Your will they existed, and were created."[41]

The bride says amen to the cherubim's holy chant. He is worthy of these things. It is right and appropriate for us to give Him this magnificent worship because He alone is Creator. *He* is responsible for all things coming into existence, not some random species adaptation over millions of years. Our God is not that small. No, His Word brought all these things into being, creating from nothing universes, galaxies, constellations, stars, solar systems, and planets.[42] Space and time. Animals and air. Plants and people. From the galactic to the microscopic, they all exist because of Him and for Him.[43] The very reason for all things is to give Him honor, glory, and praise. Even unbelievers who suffer eternal wrath will eventually acknowledge His greatness.[44] How much more do you and I exist for His pleasure and praise!

This is a truth so deep it is rarely ever discussed among Christians. If we could simply get our eyes off ourselves long enough to contemplate reality as God defines it, we just might awaken from our self-induced slumber and enter a whole new level of living.

So why is Jesus revealing this heavenly scene to John? Why follow up the seven messages to the church with a peek into heaven's throne room?

I believe Jesus wanted His bride to see what John saw because He knew it would give her a distinct advantage in living down here. Think about it: beginning in chapter 6, Jesus will unveil the awful judgments of the Tribulation. He wanted His church to know (through chapter 4) that she would already be in heaven prior to

God's wrath being unleashed on earth. But second, He also gives her another promise of hope until that redemption day arrives. We already know the Holy Spirit is our "promise" and "pledge," guaranteeing us that Jesus will make good on His promise to give us our heavenly inheritance.[45] Like an engagement ring, the Holy Spirit is our present promise pointing to a future reality and fulfillment.

But through this heavenly preview, Jesus also gives us comfort, peace, rest, and security. These are a part of those awesome benefits from God I alluded to earlier. It's not ultimately why we love God. It's just a part of the benefit package that comes with being His bride. Jesus has obligated Himself to us in so many ways, simply because of how wonderful He is! Therefore, there really is a payoff in the *right now*, something that sustains us in the midst of our present pain and perseverance. While walking through the turmoil and struggle inherent with living in this dark world, we do not despair. While hostility toward Jesus and His bride continues to increase, and while evil, violence, godlessness, immorality, corruption, and sin continue to rise like floodwaters, we do not fear.

As we witness the chaos in our world, it's easy to get overwhelmed. There's the constant threat of war, infectious disease, increasing hatred against believers and disregard for Judeo-Christian values, growing acceptance of homosexual marriage, imminent threat of lone-wolf terrorist attacks, ISIS terrorizing the Middle East, the spread of radical Islam, rioting in America's streets. The list could go on.

So why are we not panicking? Why do we not despair? One. Simple. Reason: There is a *throne* in heaven.

Therefore, to prepare His church and help her understand our planet's last days, Jesus takes John (and us) on a virtual tour of heaven. He knows, as we consider the cataclysmic events that "must shortly take place" (4:1) here on earth, we (like our first century brothers and sisters), are likely to grow anxious, worried, insecure, or even become filled with panic. That's why Jesus paints a dramatic contrast between what *will* transpire on earth what *is* taking place in heaven. Jesus wants His bride to know that even though all hell is about to break out on earth, heaven remains tranquil, secure, and filled with praise to a God who occupies a throne. And because of Him who reigns upon that throne, our hearts are filled not with anxiety but with awe. All is well in heaven because a Sovereign, Holy God is in charge.

If this truth is important when considering the violent judgments coming to our world, how powerful are they for us now in coping with the everyday problems we face? No matter what happens here, nothing shakes the foundations of His throne there. No matter how bad things get in this present life, nothing threatens our guaranteed safe arrival in our eternal home. That truth is precisely why the psalmist wrote,

> God is our refuge and strength,
> A very present help in trouble.
> Therefore we will not fear, though the earth should
> change
> And though the mountains slip into the heart of the
> sea.[46]

How then can we not cope, knowing this is our God? Yes, our problems and struggles, hurts and heartaches are real. But they are only for a short while.[47]

Wake up, bride! Your God is on His throne and all is well.

8

Rebels and Wrath

John's heavenly vision continues, and he sees a book (scroll) in "the right hand of Him who sat on the throne."[1] No one in heaven or on earth, living or dead, is worthy to break the seal and open the scroll. This causes John to weep, until one of the elders comforts him with the news that "the Lion that is from the tribe of Judah, the Root of David, has overcome so as to open the book and its seven seals."[2] Jesus takes the book out of the Father's hand, and when He does, another round of praise ignites from the twenty-four elders and the four living creatures. Each of them grabs a harp and golden bowls full of incense, representing the prayers of the saints.

Here are the lyrics to their new song,

> "Worthy are You to take the book and to break its seals; for You were slain, and purchased for God with Your blood men from every tribe and tongue and people and nation. You have made them to be a kingdom and priests to our God; and they will reign upon the earth."[3]

And why does heaven burst into this massive song of praise?

First, because of the enormous price Jesus paid. He was "slain," a reminder of His violent death. This tells us that even in heaven, we'll never get over His sacrifice for us.

Second, because of the scope of His redemptive work. Ever wonder who will be in heaven? According to Revelation, representatives from every nation, people group, language, and tribe will be there. Salvation reaches to the ends of the earth.[4]

But heaven's song of praise is enhanced by yet another mind-blowing fact. John looks and sees more angels and worshippers than he can possibly count. So great is their number that he simply runs out of available first-century vocabulary. John subsequently chooses the highest word in the Greek language with the largest numerical value and then simply multiplies it by itself![5]

I believe one of heaven's surprises will be the sheer number of worshippers there. You may think, *Wait, didn't Jesus say the road that leads to life is narrow and only a few find it?* Yes. But remember, since creation, a whole lot of people have lived on earth, and God's mercy is beyond comprehension. He loves humanity and is working in people's lives more than we know.

Though clearly most won't be saved, His saving grace reaches even to the smallest tribe and people group. The grace is deep. The grace is great. And heaven knows it. To this truth, we can only say with the angels, "Amen."[6]

The Fearsome Foursome

Now John transitions from heaven back to earth, from unending praise to undiluted fury. As God pours out wrath on earth and its people during the seven years following the Rapture, it's almost impossible to wrap our heads around the magnitude and intensity of His anger against mankind and its sin. Be warned: this will be a dark chapter, but one that nevertheless exalts God in His righteousness.

Seal Judgments

First Seal, First Rider (6:1-2). The Lamb breaks the first seal and a "living creature" (one of the cherubim) with a thunderous voice summons a white horse and its rider. This rider has a bow and a bestowed crown, and he goes forth conquering and to conquer. I believe this refers to Antichrist and his ability to subjugate the world in the months following the Rapture. He'll do this by providing something all humanity will crave at the moment—"peace and safety."[7] And he does so peacefully and persuasively without spilling a drop of blood. There's a fascinating parallel here between Jesus's words in Matthew 24, Luke 21, and Revelation 6–7. This man is worse than the fabled Headless Horseman. Instead, he is a *heartless* horseman.

Second Seal, Second Rider (6:3-4). Summoned by the second living creature, he rides a red horse and is given the authority to take peace from the earth (i.e., make war). The smiling, manipulative leader has now turned on the world.[8] This also mirrors the violence earth saw in the days of Noah.[9] Crime and looting will likely skyrocket during this time.

Third Seal, Third Rider (6:5-6). The third rider is called forth, riding a black horse and carrying a set of scales. Because of Antichrist's actions and war, the world will be plunged into famine and poverty. A voice, presumably Christ's, reveals to John the depths of this devastation: "A quart of wheat for a denarius, and three quarts of barley for a denarius." A denarius was a first-century day's wage. A quart of wheat was roughly equivalent to what it took to feed one person for one day. So inflation due to war (and perhaps the aftershocks of life in post-Rapture earth) will drive food prices through the roof!

I live in the South, and when one snowflake falls, people practically stampede their way to the grocery store, stocking up on food and necessities, stripping the shelves bare. Imagine the chaos and panic that ensues when multitudes can't earn enough money to feed their families or take care of other fundamental needs.[10] Food supplies won't meet the great demand, so prices skyrocket. The voice concludes with "do not damage the oil and the wine," both of which were staple foods in the first century, indicating that famine drives populations to eating only the basics.

Fourth Seal, Fourth Rider (6:8). Summoned by the fourth living creature, this horse is ashen or pale green in color, resembling the pallor of a decomposing corpse. The rider on this horse is given a name: "Death," and accompanied by "Hades." He's given authority to kill 25 percent of earth's population. This massive death toll is reached "with sword and with famine and with pestilence and by the wild beasts of the earth."[11] Though Christ holds the keys to death and Hades (1:13), He here authorizes this horseman's judgment during the Tribulation.

These four horsemen all represent effects brought on by Antichrist. And all this is merely the beginning of "birth pangs."[12]

Fifth Seal, Martyrs (6:9-11). Jesus breaks the fifth seal, and John's eyes are diverted momentarily back to heaven where he sees the souls of those who've been murdered for their faith during the Tribulation. Specifically, they're killed because of their allegiance to the Word of God and their testimony concerning Jesus.[13] These souls cry out for justice, but are told to wait a little while longer until the rest of their soon-to-be martyred brethren join them in heaven.[14]

Sixth Seal, Catastrophe (6:12-17). Here the Lord takes direct responsibility in bringing judgment on the earth. Though there have been earlier earthquakes, a massive, global seismic event now occurs.[15] This naturally triggers volcanic eruptions on a grand scale. The resulting ash spewing into the sky causes the sun to be darkened and the moon to resemble a blood-red hue.[16] Asteroids and meteors penetrate the atmosphere, colliding with the earth. Due to the massive earthquake, tectonic plates shift, realigning the earth's geography, perhaps even continents themselves.

And people's response? Both rich and poor, king and slave run for cover, even begging the mountains and the rocks to fall on them in order to shield them from "the presence of Him who sits on the throne, and from the wrath of the Lamb." There is no doubt in anyone's mind who's responsible for these events. They even know God's *motivation*. The inborn God-consciousness, present in every person, awakes to recognize that "the great day of their wrath has come, and who is able to stand?"[17] Filled with fear, they cower under rocks instead of taking shelter in the Rock of Ages.[18] Previously, they lived as if God didn't exist. But now, atheism suffers a brutal death at the hands of Jesus's wrath. This same Jesus also predicted these occurrences, stating "there will be terrors and great signs from heaven."[19]

Pause for Praise

Chapter 7 presses the pause button in the Revelation narrative, switching scenes once again. John sees four angels placed at four strategic locations on the earth. Another angel rises up, commanding the others to supernaturally suspend God's judgment for a brief period of time. The reason? The Lord commissions an elite corps of "End-Times Evangelists," placing His seal of protection, ownership, and identification on their foreheads.[20] This chosen group is numbered at 144,000 and are 100 percent Jewish.[21] From Revelation 14 we also discover they remain sexually pure, maintain moral integrity, and are protected from harm throughout the Tribulation.[22] They're described as *sealed* (7:3,4,8), *servants* (7:3), *purchased* (14:3-4), *followers* of the Lamb (14:4), and *first fruits* (14:4).

From this description a portrait emerges, giving every indication that these young Jewish males are the very first to embrace faith in the Messiah during the Tribulation, at least among Jews. They are bondservants to Christ, spreading the message of His salvation. And their ministry is very fruitful.

John continues revealing to the bride what he sees in heaven. There, standing before God's throne is an innumerable multitude of saved individuals from "every nation and all tribes and peoples and tongues." This is the same group we saw in Revelation 6:9, and answers the question posed by those hiding from God's wrath in 6:17, "their wrath has come, and who is able to stand?" God responds in 7:9, telling us the redeemed are "standing" before the throne in worship. Those who ultimately stand are those who bow before this King of heaven. Jesus withstood God's wrath against sin so we could one day stand before His throne.

But this scene tells us more than just the scope of the evangelists' ministry.[23] It also answers the skeptic's question, "What about those who have never heard?" As Jesus prophesied many years earlier, His gospel will be preached to the ends of the earth before the end comes.[24] The saved multitude in Revelation 7:13-14 has come *out of* the Tribulation. This massive, redeemed throng is now enjoying their righteousness, celebrating and crying out to God. And their worship transitions them from being on their feet to falling on their faces before the throne.

John also lets us know that their suffering is officially over. Evidently, they were hungry, thirsty, and exposed to the elements as they attempted to survive along with the rest of humanity during Tribulation's judgments. Their suffering also likely refers to their refusal to take the "mark of the beast."[25] However, now they're comforted by the presence of their Savior and Shepherd as they drink from the water of life and have their tears wiped away by Him (vv. 16-17).

This important chapter informs the bride of several key truths.

1. *God is not finished with the Jewish people.* No doubt many in the crowd John sees in heaven are of Jewish descent, brought to their promised Messiah by the 144,000. Who better to reach and relate to a Jew than a fellow Jew?

2. *Jews and Gentiles, though united in the church age and in heaven, are seen as separate during the Tribulation.* God doesn't raise up 144,000 *Gentile* evangelists. This is because, having temporarily

set Israel aside during the church age, He circles back to deal with individual Jews and national Israel during this end-times period.[26]

3. Will people be saved during the Tribulation? The answer is yes! Massive numbers of people from all over the world will believe.[27] However, salvation will cost them dearly, with many losing their lives through beheading.[28] John's mention of beheading has caused many to wonder exactly how this hideous brand of execution will be reintroduced during the Tribulation. But consider his first-century context, where Rome used the sword to execute those it deemed worthy of death. Such was the case with James, the first apostle to be martyred in Acts 12:1.

Today, we're seeing a resurgence of this barbaric practice through radical Islam. This very week, someone will likely have their head hacked or sawed off by this satanically inspired religious group. Beheading is back, my friend. And it will be the official chosen method of killing Christians in that day.

Even so, vast numbers will come to Christ at this time. Aren't you amazed at the compassionate heart of our Savior? Up to the last moment, people will still be given the chance to be saved. Most will continue hardening their hearts, just as they did before. But many others will be convinced of their need for salvation and run to the cross.[29]

Intermission is over, and John's attention now turns to the seventh seal. Jesus breaks open this seal, which initiates thirty minutes of silent anticipation in heaven followed by repeated thunder and lightning and an earthquake.[30] This seventh seal initiates seven more judgments, each one announced by a trumpet blast from one of the seven angels who stand before God.

Blasts of Wrath

The Trumpet Judgments are round two of God's wrath unleashed upon the earth. Some believe that, while the Seal Judgments are delivered in the first half of the Tribulation, both the Trumpet and

Bowl Judgments occur during the second three and a half years.[31] Though their sequential order is clear, it's too speculative to try and pinpoint the exact timing of these during the Tribulation. Even so, let's get an overview of what happens when God's seven angels blow their trumpets.

Trumpet Blast One (8:7). Hail, fire, and blood rain down from the sky, perhaps resulting from the angel-induced earthquake in verse 5. Lava spews into the atmosphere, raining down "red fire."[32] One third of the earth and trees are burned up, including all the green grass. Can you even imagine this?

Trumpet Blast Two (8:8-9). A massive, fiery "meteor mountain" descends from the heavens, crashing into the sea and turning a third of the oceans to blood. One-third of sea life dies and an equal percentage of ships are destroyed.

Trumpet Blast Three (8:10-11). A "star" (perhaps a comet or asteroid) falls from the sky, "burning like a torch," breaking up and contaminating a third of rivers and springs of waters as it hits the earth. This object is given a name—Wormwood—and many, desperately thirsty, drink from this bitter water supply and die.[33]

Trumpet Blast Four (8:12). The earth's light sources (sun, moon, and stars) are temporarily dimmed by one third their illuminating power.[34] Imagine the impact this loss of heat will have on the earth and its inhabitants. It's climate change on steroids!

A brief interlude occurs here (8:13). An angel hovering in the sky (pictured as an eagle)[35] announces the first of three "woes" directed at those who dwell on the earth. A "woe" is a warning of impending grief or suffering and here points to more severe judgments. It's God's way of saying, "You haven't seen anything yet. It's about to get a lot worse."

Trumpet Blast Five (9:1-12). In this first woe, a "star," here a fallen angel (possibly Satan), takes a key, opening "the bottomless pit" containing a vile brand of demonic creatures.[36] It's possible these demons include those who cohabited with mortal women in the days of Noah, prompting God to keep them in chains for over five thousand years.[37]

These hideous creatures appear as locusts with stinger tails like scorpions. For *five straight months* they are given authority to torment mankind, but those who have God's seal of salvation on them are protected. Their strike is compared to a scorpion's painful sting. They're like horses prepared for battle, with man-faces and golden crown-like headgear. They have lions' teeth and long hair. Their breastplates are like iron, and the collective swarming sound of their wings resembles charging horses or chariots rushing to battle. They are filled with fury and hatred for God and the human beings He made in His image. Their fulfillment and pleasure is found in tormenting humanity. These scorpion-locust demons attack at will in a full-on torture-frenzy. The physical pain and psychological horror is so intense that people will beg to die but won't be able to.[38] It's a foretaste of hell as both suicide and relief are denied them. A king called the "angel of the abyss" leads these demons. In Hebrew his name is *Abaddon*. In Greek, *Apollyon*. In English, *Destroyer*.

Sound fun? That's just the first of three woes.

Trumpet Blast Six (9:13-21). At the start of this second woe, John hears a voice coming from the altar before God commanding the sixth angel to release four demons who've been bound at the Euphrates River.[39] Held captive specifically for this exact day, these four devils are released upon the earth.[40] So sovereign is our God, He even uses demons to fulfill His righteous purposes. Their mission—to kill another third of mankind. This now accounts for a little more than half of the earth's population being destroyed![41] Not since the days of Noah has God poured out such wrath on humanity. These four foul generals gather to lead an army numbered at two hundred million. Yes, you read that right. Two hundred million.

In fact, John reaffirms this fact by saying he actually "heard" the number with his own ears.[42] There have been several interpretations as to exactly who this army is. Many have suggested it refers to

China, since that country has for decades boasted of fielding a military force this size. But though in Scripture God has previously used human armies to accomplish His purposes, these don't appear to be ordinary horses as they're associated with demons. This mounted cavalry are wearing supernatural armor of fire, sulfur, and brimstone.[43] These fire-breathing demon horses have tails like serpents, and with them they do harm to mankind.

And what about those who survive the attack of these hellish horsemen? In a clear display of the human heart's wickedness, amazingly they do not repent,[44] even when confronted with God's repeated judgments.[45] Shades of Pharaoh, right? Though half the world is destroyed, they're not convinced of their need for salvation. Instead, they harden their hearts and continue "to worship demons" and inanimate, mute idols made of gold, silver, brass, stone, and wood.

Veneration of man-made idols is often associated with demonic worship.[46] This highlights the fact that we're all natural-born worshippers. We simply cannot *not* worship something, but rather irresistibly pursue what gives us a perceived sense of meaning, identity, love, or comfort. And a darkened, hardened, godless heart will seek those things through the most corrupt means possible. This is why God's first commandment under Moses's leadership was, "You shall have no other gods before Me," immediately followed by "You shall not make for yourself an idol...You shall not worship them or serve them."[47]

For all our technology and sophistication, left alone we are simply powerless to rise above our inborn paganism. Humanity in the end times will not have moved beyond its ancient counterpart. Whether living in a desert tent four thousand years ago or in a high-rise condo in 2015, not much has changed about us. Both then and now, we naturally resist God and embrace darkness.[48] Though some during the Tribulation may initially exhibit respectable religiosity, it also appears there will be a strong resurgence in the worship of demonic entities. Allegiance to these demons is visually represented here through sculpted or carved representations made of stone, wood, and precious metals.

With God's Restrainer absent during this time, demons will have a field day, unchecked and unimpeded by the Holy Spirit working through the bride. As a result, their influence and ability to oppress humans will exponentially increase. It's ironic that these remaining earth-dwellers worship the very demons who bring some of their pain and suffering. Such is the deceptive trickery of sin, Satan, and the human heart. And it's the ultimate slavery. In short, sin makes people stupid.

Additionally, mankind also stubbornly refuses to repent of other sins, specifically *murder, sorcery, immorality,* and *theft.* In a world gone mad, men and women desperately reach out for anything for survival and satisfaction. In the Tribulation, the murder rate will soar as a spirit of chaos envelopes the world.

The word translated "sorceries" here is the Greek *pharmakon* and can refer to anything from poisons, amulets, charms, drugs, magic spells, witchcraft, or any enchanting object.[49] Drugs were heavily used in first-century sorcery, inducing a psychological state conducive to trances for contacting departed or demonic spirits. This practice will become prevalent in the last days.[50] Today, drug abuse is at an alarming level. We escape through drugs—alcohol, marijuana, cocaine, meth, heroine, and a host of legally prescribed pharmaceuticals—becoming a "medication nation." Drugs dull the pain, causing us to temporarily forget our problems and our life condition.

As our world races toward Revelation, expect to see drug use and abuse continue to rise and become legalized. And in the turmoil and madness of the Tribulation, it will become epidemic. People will seek to escape into a drug-bunker of protection from the world outside their door, retreating into an insulated, hallucinogenic, mind-numbing haze.

They will also practice unrestrained *immorality,* just as they did in Noah's day and in Sodom and Gomorrah.[51] Sexual taboos will be removed, if not officially, at least in the public psyche. With no bride to represent Scripture's morality, rape, pedophilia, and homosexuality will combine with a host of other sexual sins to soak the earth in defilement. We're already way down this path, and some are now even pushing for acts such as pedophilia to be decriminalized, reclassifying these people from "perverts" to "minor attracted" individuals.[52] It's simply their particular sexual orientation, they claim. This is setting the stage, preparing what's left of the human race for utter decadence in the end times.[53]

Rounding out this list of sins that mankind refuses to repent of is *theft*. The Tribulation's crime wave will reach tsunami-like proportions. Lawlessness will run rampant in the streets. We've seen what happens when angry protestors unleash their wrath on America's city shops and stores. However, the looting and thievery described here will make situations like Ferguson, Missouri, and Baltimore seem like a church picnic. Anarchy fills the earth, and no home or individual will be safe. "What's yours is mine!" is the new Main Street mantra.

Demon worship. Idolatry. Murders. Sorceries. Immorality. Thefts.

This is the weather forecast for humanity in the Tribulation's latter half. Mankind clings to these sins for survival and security, vehemently refusing to repent. By doing so, they expose themselves to a violent spirit of hatred toward God that we'll see later in Revelation.[54] This then is the deceptive danger of harboring a hard heart toward God.[55]

One Scroll, Two Witnesses, and a War

In the vision in Revelation 10, recorded exclusively for Jesus's bride, John witnesses a strong angel coming down from heaven. In his hand is a "little book" containing a mystery.[56] His voice is as a lion's roar, and is followed by seven peals of thunder announcing a message John is forbidden to even write down.[57] For now, only John will know it. This strong angel describes God as eternal Creator, declaring that the remaining judgments will now be dispensed without delay. He adds that the seventh trumpet will finish the mystery relating to the establishment of God's kingdom (previously preached to His servants the prophets).

John is then commanded to *eat* the little scroll, whose flavor begins sweet but ends up bitter. Then, as now, God's Word is both delightful and disturbing.[58] Following this, John is recommissioned to write down the rest of the revelation he is about to receive.[59]

During the Tribulation, Revelation 11 tells us God will also send "Two Witnesses" who will prophesy and perform wonders for 1260 days or three and a half years. Many see a parallel between these two and the ministries of Moses and Elijah, suggesting they, along with the 144,000 young Jewish gospel preachers, are brought back to earth to assist in converting Jews. Following their mission, these two are killed by the Antichrist. Their dead bodies are put on display in Jerusalem's streets as the world celebrates, even exchanging gifts over the festive occasion of their deaths. It's like New Year's Eve at Times Square. But after three and a half days, God breathes life into them, and they stand on their feet and ascend to heaven in the sight of their enemies. This is followed by a great earthquake that devastates a portion of the city, killing seven thousand.

Bowl Season

Are you overwhelmed yet? Out of breath? Have these prophetic truths pricked you like a cactus plant on our climb up this mountain? Do you feel their sting? Do you sense the unpleasantness associated with these future judgments? It would take a book much thicker than this one to thoroughly cover every detail recorded in Revelation. But we're hitting the important mountain peaks, giving you a clear panorama of end-times events and their significance for your life now. With such prophecy, it's easy to get lost in the details and miss the big picture. So stay alert.

Now back to the trail and our climb.

Preceding the next round of judgments is yet another interlude in Revelation 11:15-19. Among other reasons, this pause allows John and the bride to catch their breath in what has been a wild prophetic roller-coaster ride. These verses also provide spiritual comfort, assuring us that God is subduing earthly kingdoms and that His Christ will reign forever.

We previously saw that the Sixth Trumpet is synonymous with the second of three woes. *The Seventh Trumpet Blast (11:15-19)* then signals the third woe and the beginning of the Seven Bowl Judgments. The increasing frequency of these bowl judgments in Tribulation's final three and a half years leads up to Jesus's ultimate return, coronation, and kingdom. [60] In keeping with the continuity of the Bowl Judgments, we're fast-forwarding to Revelation 16 where John picks up his description of these Judgments. Revelation 12–15 is addressed elsewhere in this chapter, as well as in chapter 8.

The First Bowl (16:1-2). A "loud" (Greek, *mega*) voice, undoubtedly God's, commands one of the seven angels to "pour out on the earth...the wrath of God." [61] This judgment comes in the form of a painful, malignant sore on all those who had the "mark of the beast." A similar plague of boils was visited on the Egyptians in Exodus 9:9-11. [62]

The Second Bowl (16:3). The sea becomes blood, killing "every living thing" in it. [63] This also appears to parallel one of the ten plagues of Egypt. [64] Imagine the putrid odor this event brings inland.

The Third Bowl (16:4-7). Rivers and springs of water become blood. This judgment is payback, specifically administered because "they poured out the blood of saints and prophets." During the

Tribulation an unholy holocaust will take place with the slaughter and beheading of thousands of believers. God says to those who participated in this gruesome activity, "Since you enjoy pouring out the blood of My people, blood is exactly what you will drink." Believers take comfort in knowing God will bring justice for every drop of Christian martyr blood spilt. It's a terrible judgment on these murderers, and yet the third angel's words remind us, "They deserve it" (v. 6). And the prayers of slaughtered saints are finally answered (cf. 6:9-11).

The Fourth Bowl (16:8-9). Whereas the sun's intensity was dimmed with the Fourth Trumpet Judgment, here it greatly increases. Scorching men with "fierce heat," there is no relief from the oppressive, searing temperature. If global in its reach, this judgment would presumably melt the polar ice caps, causing the world's oceans to rise by over two hundred feet.[65] In this scenario, all of Florida disappears under a bloody sea of death. However, instead of repenting, mankind blasphemes the God who sent this judgment.

The Fifth Bowl (16:10-11). Previously, part of the atmosphere was darkened by the smoke from the bottomless pit of demons (9:2). Here the entire kingdom of Antichrist is covered in darkness, again reminiscent of Egypt's plagues.[66] The psychological effect of this darkness is so unnerving that people actually "gnaw their tongues" in torment. And yet, so hardened are their hearts that they again "blasphemed the God of heaven" (v. 11).

The Sixth Bowl (16:12-16). The great River Euphrates is dried up in preparation for armies from the east.[67] It's unclear whether their intent is to overthrow Antichrist's kingdom due to disillusionment with or to attack a defiant Jerusalem. Regardless, they eventually find themselves battling the captain of the Lord of Hosts. God, having previously demonstrated to the Egyptians and the Jews His ability to dry up a sea, paves the way for their battle approach.[68]

In conjunction with this, three "unclean spirits like frogs" spew forth from the mouths of Satan, the beast, and the false prophet. These demons perform supernatural signs summoning the world's kings and their military forces together "for the war of the great day of God, the Almighty" (v. 14). Though their chances of winning this war are nil, these foul spirits are deluded by their sin-fueled arrogance. This final God-war is the culmination of several previous battles, leading to a climactic conflict.[69]

But just before the final Bowl Judgment is poured out, Jesus makes an important announcement: "Behold, I am coming like a thief. Blessed is the one who *stays awake* and keeps his clothes, so that he will not walk about naked and men will not see his shame."[70] To believers still alive at this time, Jesus says, "Be alert. Keep the faith. I'm returning soon."

The three demons successfully gather the world's armies to a place that in Hebrew is called Har-Magedon.[71] The apostle prepares us to encounter the return of Christ as we now approach the end of the Great Tribulation.

The Seventh Bowl (16:17-21). This final Bowl Judgment portrays earth's final hours, which leads all the way up to Jesus' Second Coming. God punctuates the end of His judgments with history's most devastating earthquake (16:18). This violent event radically alters earth's topography, with the city of Babylon receiving a special fermented dose of God's fury (16:19-20). This is followed by 100-pound hailstones raining down from the sky, causing unparalleled destruction (16:21). And yet, even then, men continue to curse and blaspheme God. Unbelievable.

We've seen God's response to a rebellious planet. But before we descend into the Valley of Megiddo and Armageddon, Jesus wants His bride to know about the one Satan chooses to spearhead his final diabolical drive for world domination.

Are you ready to unmask Antichrist?

9

Satan's Celebrity

Old Testament believers were privileged to see certain far-off prophetic mountain peaks and yet still not understand their distance from them or what valleys or plains lay in between. It's the same with us. At times, it can get a bit confusing and unclear. But that's often the nature of prophetic Scripture. However, like a distant road sign, what's difficult to make out becomes clearer the closer we get to it. And so we travel on, encountering now what is perhaps the creepiest part of Revelation.

War in Heaven

In Revelation 12, John is given a glimpse of the past as well as the future. He witnesses a woman giving birth to a child who is about to be devoured by a "great red dragon." But the child is "caught up" to heaven, thwarting the dragon's intentions.[1] Though some see this woman as Mary, both the immediate and historical context clearly point to her identity as Israel and the child as Christ.[2] The dragon is Satan, and his original revolt in heaven is described as he, along with one-third of the angels, are thrown to earth.[3]

John then fast-forwards from the birth and ascension of Jesus (vv. 3-5) to the Tribulation (vv. 6-17). At the midpoint of the seven-year

Tribulation, it appears Antichrist will begin another holocaust-like persecution of the Jewish people. Verses 6 and 13-17 tell us Israel will flee for safety into the wilderness to a place God prepares for her. There, He will take care of her for 1260 days (three and a half years).[4] Verse 17 states these are Jews who have believed in Jesus as Messiah, representing one-third of all Israel.[5]

Around this same time, John witnesses a war in heaven (vv. 7-12). Satan musters his demonic armies in an effort to once again dethrone God.[6] In this cosmic coup attempt, the archangel Michael and his holy angels fight the evil intruders and win, throwing all of them back down to earth. This is not Michael's first rodeo with the devil, having previously battled him over the dead body of Moses.[7] This humiliating defeat infuriates the devil and lets him know his ultimate demise is soon to come.[8]

For centuries, Satan has perpetually accused believers, having been granted access before God's throne.[9] But following this episode, all future admittance is denied.[10] Therefore Satan becomes desperate, insane with revengeful rage. This explains in part why he goes after believing Israel so vehemently in the Tribulation's second half. But that's only the outward expression of his wrath. His real motivation is a boiling hatred toward God Himself. It's a loathing hostility that cannot be understood by us or changed by the Lord.

The devil is doomed, and he knows it. Even so, he continues acting out his character as portrayed by his names—dragon (terrifying beast), serpent of old (deceiver), devil (slanderer, accuser) and Satan (adversary). Upon his final expulsion by Michael and his angelic army, all heaven celebrates.[11]

Wouldn't you?

History's Mystery Man

Body slammed to earth by God's mighty archangel, Satan is filled with fury and foul-mouthed rants. Returning to his game plan for ruling the world, he calls up a diabolical secret weapon from the sea of humanity.[12] It's a man, called by Scripture what he really is—the beast[13]—and he lives up to the title. He is known by other names as well, among them:

- the prince who is to come (Daniel 9:26)
- the king who does as he pleases (Daniel 11:36-45)
- the man of lawlessness (2 Thessalonians 2:3)
- the son of destruction (2 Thessalonians 2:3)
- the little horn (Daniel 7:8)
- the rider on a white horse (Revelation 6:2)

But those are relatively obscure names compared to the one we're most familiar with: *Antichrist.*[14]

The very word evokes images of sinister movie portrayals and a faceless evil persona. He is history's mystery man. The ultimate villainous VIP. The devil with skin on. Of course, the *spirit* of Antichrist is alive today, having been at work since the first century.[15] But this spirit finds its ultimate embodiment in the beast. He is simultaneously the antithesis of Jesus Christ and an imposter Messiah. Like his master, the dragon, he's an inventor of lies.[16]

However, we must be careful not to go beyond the boundary of Scripture when making definitive statements about Antichrist. Assumptions about him must not be equated with absolute truth, though informed opinions can be entertained if they're anchored to God's Word. But we have to delineate between what we know and what is still unclear. While it's impossible to know the identity and all the specifics of Antichrist prior to the Rapture, the Bible does give us an emerging profile. We have a defined outline, a darkened silhouette, but not a face. So what do we actually know?

This man is not only "anti" Christ, but within that role he also mimics or imitates the Messiah. For example, like Revelation's portrayal of Jesus, Antichrist also possesses a symbolic sword and horns, is slain and resurrected, and marks his followers with a name.[17] To be clear, no human ruler in history has *ever* fulfilled all the prophecies concerning Antichrist. So although we cannot know his exact identity or name, we can know he's coming, what he is like, and what he will do.

When searching for a crime suspect, law enforcement gathers intelligence and compiles a character sketch of the person. A suspect profile. Fortunately, in the case of Antichrist, Scripture does that work for us.

But first, Jesus thought it important for His bride to know a bit about Antichrist's place in history's big picture. John sees him as having "ten horns and seven heads, and on his horns were ten diadems, and on his head were blasphemous names."[18] Don't be too freaked out by that bizarre description. The Lord could have left us in the dark about these things, but He wanted His church and those who embrace Him during the Tribulation to have an idea of what was going on. As it turns out, the symbolism here is not as difficult as you might think.

The ten horns represent ten kingdoms.[19] We can discern this because the prophecies of Daniel 7 parallel many of the events we see taking place during the Tribulation. Daniel 7:24 states that a future world leader (Antichrist) will have authority over a ten-nation coalition. We don't know exactly who these nations will be, but the beast will be the leader among them.[20] Many Bible scholars believe this ten-nation kingdom will be a revival of the ancient Roman Empire.[21]

Daniel 7 contains a vision regarding four kingdoms. Each is personified as a type of beast representing a world empire. With the hindsight of history, we can now easily identify these four world kingdoms.

1. Babylon—a lion with wings of an eagle (Daniel 7:4)

2. Medo-Persia—a lopsided bear with three ribs in its mouth (Daniel 7:5)

3. Greece—a leopard with four wings and four heads (Daniel 7:6)

4. Rome—a terrible beast with teeth of iron and claws of bronze (Daniel 7:7)

Daniel's prophecies concerning these four empires were all literally fulfilled. However, there is a prophecy regarding the Roman Empire that remains unfulfilled. Daniel 7:7-8 describes a final form of the Roman Empire that will emerge in the end times. This is what we see in Revelation 13. Keep in mind, contextually John is writing to believers living under a Roman government that persecutes followers of Jesus. This first-century context would help Revelation's readers better understand and grasp the prophecies regarding a future version of such an empire.

Revelation confirms that a single, global empire will arise in the end times prior to Christ's return.[22] This final form (revival) of the Roman Empire is said to have "ten horns," interpreted for us by Daniel to be ten kings or kingdoms.[23] In this final phase of the revived Roman Empire, a "little horn" will rise out of these ten kingdoms.[24] Three of these kingdom's leaders will resist the "little horn," and they are subsequently removed and replaced.[25] Eventually, all ten kingdoms submit to Antichrist's authority.[26]

The "seven heads" are interpreted for us in Revelation 17. They are seven kings (kingdoms), "five have fallen, one is, the other has not yet come." From John's first-century perspective, here's how it breaks down:

- "five have fallen"—Egypt, Babylon, Assyria, Medo-Persia, Greece (all in the past)
- "one is"—Rome (currently in John's day)

- "the other has not yet come"—Final (revived) Roman Empire headed by Antichrist (appears in the future)[27]

Many have surmised that the existing European Union most resembles the political structure and economic cooperation characteristic of Scripture's description of Antichrist's kingdom. If this is the case, the EU's scope would need to extend beyond Europe. Further, some countries may consolidate power for it to be made up of only ten kingdoms. This is not unreasonable to imagine, given that economic disaster will strike the world following the Rapture, dictating that nations come together for survival.

However, it's also possible Antichrist's kingdom is comprised of an entirely new and different entity. But what is very interesting about this kingdom being a revived Roman Empire is that when the EU was initially formed in 1957, its charter document was called "The Treaty of Rome."[28] In all of history, Rome has never been comprised of a ten-king "league of nations," especially one destroyed by Christ's kingdom.[29] That's another reason to see Revelation as future, unfulfilled prophecy.

So we can discern that a final world empire will be led by a satanically empowered individual presenting himself as a counterfeit Christ. And it's Satan who gives his chosen man the kingdoms of the world. Antichrist then personifies a "panoramic representation of dominant world empires of all time."[30] Satan previously claimed control of the world's kingdoms when he offered them to Jesus, along with all their glory. As it turns out, this was a legitimate offer.[31] But while Christ rejected this proposal, Antichrist will embrace it.[32] The "ten diadems"[33] most likely represent the kings of the ten-nation kingdom headed by Antichrist. All ten derive their authority from the beast and relinquish their power to him, uniting to support him.[34] This gives fresh insight into Scripture's bold claim about Jesus Christ being "King of kings and Lord of lords."[35]

Hallelujah!

Obviously, these prophecies require study in both Old and New Testaments, along with some understanding of history. There is much to know, including details we won't cover in this book. However, I trust that as we carefully navigate through the rocks, thorns, and perilous plants in our journey up the mountain of Revelation's prophecy, you're getting a feel for where history is headed.

So this beast, clearly a man, will be a powerful world leader. The devil's diplomat. But what else does the Bible tell us about this man?

Profiling the Antichrist

He will likely be a Gentile (Revelation 13:1). Antichrist will come "out of the sea" of humanity. This symbolic use of "sea" points to Gentile nations.[36] He is also described as rising from the "abyss" or the "deep," signifying his satanic connections.[37] Further evidence he is not Jewish is that he reigns over a Gentile empire. He also persecutes Jews, invades Israel, and desecrates the temple. Historically, only Gentiles have done similar things.

He will not be religious (Daniel 11:37). Scripture indicates he will not honor any religion or religious tradition. Some believe the phrase "he will show no regard...for the desire of women" signifies that Antichrist will either be homosexual or asexual (no sexual attraction to either gender). He will instead honor a "god of fortresses," or military power and control over the earth.[38]

His identity will be revealed following the Rapture. The Bible is clear concerning the *timing* of Antichrist's "coming out," saying that this "man of lawlessness" will not be revealed until after "he who now restrains...is taken out of the way."[39] I believe the identity of this powerful "restrainer" is the Holy Spirit who indwells all believers (the church). When the bride is taken away at the Rapture, so will the restraining influence of the Holy Spirit, who presently holds back a tsunami of sin, which will flood the earth in the end times. Therefore, the identity of the Antichrist cannot be known until sometime after the Rapture.

However, considering the global panic that will grip earth's inhabitants following this shocking event, those who remain will need a strong leader who can bring relative calm to a distraught humanity. This will be just the type of crisis the opportunistic beast will be waiting for. Similar to Hitler in prewar Germany, he will capitalize on this crisis, manipulating a desperate population. He will seize upon the chance to position himself onto the world scene in a place of prominence and global influence. Again, it makes sense in this post-Rapture scenario that his initial platform will be one of "peace and safety."[40]

He will be a charismatic influencer (Daniel 7:8,11; 11:36; Revelation 13:2,5). Today, millions blindly follow faux celebrities. Without thinking, we pledge our allegiance to empty-suit politicians making equally empty promises. What will the mass of humanity do when the most mesmerizing man in history hypnotizes them with his demonic charm and influence? He is everything a godless, secular world has ever wanted—a man who can deliver peace, economic hope, political leadership, and a globally uniting alternative to Christianity.

He will lead the world into a global economy (Daniel 11:43; Revelation 13:16-17). This gets the world's attention and puts Antichrist on the map, making him the most powerful man on the planet. How he initially does this is not known, but it may have something to do with uniting the nations following the Rapture. As worldwide economic disaster strikes following this event, the consolidating of countries for mutual survival and benefit could be a way to temporarily save the planet from an economic nosedive. Eventually, Antichrist will control who buys and sells.[41] In times of crisis, people historically surrender personal freedoms for promised financial rescue.

He will broker a peace treaty with Israel, but later break it (Daniel 9:27; 12:11; Revelation 6:2). Antichrist will do what every American president in recent history has dreamed of—bringing peace to the Middle East. It's possible he will either orchestrate a cease-fire between Israel and Palestine or somehow strike a deal between Jews and Muslims regarding the Temple Mount area, allowing Israel to rebuild the temple. He could do both, causing his political clout and stock to soar. This peace treaty makes it possible for the first time in two thousand years for Jews to offer sacrifices in a rebuilt temple in Jerusalem.

Interestingly, The Temple Institute, an organization founded in 1987, is dedicated to rebuilding that temple. They've already fashioned sacred temple vessels and priestly garments according to exact Old Testament specifications.[42] They are simply waiting for construction to one day begin. I believe the Antichrist will play a key role in making that temple construction possible. But it's all just another devilish deception, as Antichrist has ulterior motives.

He will be killed but rise from the dead (Revelation 13:3-14; 17:8). At some point, likely around the midpoint of the first three and a half years of the Tribulation, Antichrist will suffer a "fatal wound" inflicted by a "sword." We do not know the exact nature of this event, but John sees the wound as violent and deadly.[43] There is every indication to suggest this is a real death, not a faked one (though that would be consistent with Satan's deceptive character). This is another attempt to parallel the real Christ as Antichrist mimics and mocks the death and resurrection of Jesus.

If there was any doubt in anyone's mind as to the supernatural nature of this man, this event dispels those doubts. This resurrection event will rocket the beast's fame and power to an all-time high, and he wastes no time capitalizing on it. With the aid of his right-hand man, he secures for himself worldwide admiration, allegiance, and worship as "the whole earth was amazed and followed after the beast." The entire world goes gaga over their new god. Revelation 13:4 tells us that ultimately their worship is directed toward the dragon (Satan).[44] This has been Lucifer's vision and objective ever since his initial heavenly rebellion.[45] The wonder and awe produced by Satan's power on behalf of Antichrist is what initiates this worship. The greater the awe, the greater the worship.

The same is true for believers. Ever wonder why Christians are often lethargic in worship? Why our allegiance is weak and our obedience sporadic? It's because we know little of God's power working through the church. Imagine how our faith and worship would explode if we witnessed more of God's life-changing work in the lives of His people. Again, the spiritual principle here is "the greater the awe, the greater the worship."

As a result of this resurrection miracle, earth's inhabitants express their worship toward Antichrist, saying, "Who is like the beast, and who is able to wage war with him?"[46] This ascribing of glory directly parallels declarations made about Yahweh.[47] "Who is like the beast?" According to the whole world, the answer is "No one!" He is unique and stands unequalled. He has no peers. And he knows it. Paul wrote of his arrogance, "He will exalt himself and defy everything that people call god and every object of worship. He will even sit in the temple of God, claiming that he himself is God."[48]

Because he has successfully defeated death, his military power is now unquestioned. "Who is able to wage war with the beast?" The actual answer to this is found a little later in Revelation 17:14 and 19:11-21. But for now the entire world exalts this satanic celebrity above all mankind, elevating him to godlike status. Ah, the plan is working. They're taking the dragon's bait, and he's reeling them all in like helpless fish.

He will desecrate the temple, declaring himself to be God (Matthew 24:15; Revelation 11:2; 13:5-15; Daniel 7:8; 2 Thessalonians 2:4). Until this point, Antichrist has allowed religions to coexist, but at Tribulation's midpoint he declares himself to be God. This is what Christ called the "Abomination of Desolation," as Antichrist sits in the Jewish temple as God. Later, a likeness of him is placed there for all the world to worship.[49] This Abomination compels a number of believing Jews to escape into the wilderness to a place prepared for them there by God.[50] But now that Antichrist requires the entire world to worship him, most of the world's inhabitants do so willingly in light of his godlike ability to rise from the dead.[51]

He will make war with the saints (Revelation 13:7). Many will trust Christ after the Rapture and during Antichrist's reign. However, they will pay dearly for their loyalty to Jesus. Antichrist will have believers hunted down, arrested, thrown in prison, and executed.[52] Aside from Christians, there won't be a single person who doesn't worship the beast. Only those whose names have been written down in the "book of life of the Lamb who has been slain" will resist him.[53] The names of the redeemed were written down in this heavenly book "from the foundation of the world." This tells us our redemption is older than creation itself, and that God's loving heart and will to save us traces to eternity past.[54] That's how long God has loved you.

This persecution is directed at those who believe in Jesus during the Tribulation, and excludes the bride, as she's already been raptured.[55] John tells us God's sovereignty is the truth fueling the perseverance and faithfulness of these persecuted believers.[56]

He is a man of unimaginable blasphemy (Revelation 13:5). Antichrist's pride and self-love is matched only by his intense hatred of God. He despises Yahweh, evidenced by his constant efforts to mock Him through duplicating a messianic persona. He constantly ridicules and scoffs at the person of God, His name, and those who dwell in heaven.[57] Being human, you and I can experience only human hatred. But Antichrist's animosity toward God is supernatural, as it is energized by Satan himself. It is a foul fury that spews forth from his lying lips. And the same Satan that empowers him seeks to devour you right now. Therefore, be on the alert.[58]

He is accompanied by the false prophet (Revelation 13:11-18). This is the last member of Satan's three-pronged attack against God. He is called "another beast," meaning "another of the same kind." He possesses the same evil nature and empowerment as the first beast

(Antichrist). He is also called "the false prophet."[59] Jesus warned, "For false Christs and false prophets will arise and will show great signs and wonders, so as to mislead, if possible, even the elect."[60]

Though many have existed since the first century, this man is *the* false prophet with the first beast being *the* false Christ. He speaks with the voice of a dragon, meaning he's the mouthpiece of Antichrist, powered by Satan. He promotes Antichrist like a campaign manager, fulfilling his evil agenda, playing a similar role as the Holy Spirit does in the ministry of Christ.[61] He possesses the power to work satanic signs and convincing miracles, even calling down fire from heaven. Like his dark lord, he too is a master deceiver, leading the earth into worship of the beast.[62] This demonstrates that even someone performing (or experiencing) a supposed miracle is not sufficient reason to authenticate that person as being from God. Instead, we are to carefully "test the spirits" using the Word of God.[63] Satan will perform supernatural signs during the Tribulation, so it's no surprise he'd do the same today as he "disguises himself as an angel of light."[64]

The false prophet is the ultimate wolf in sheep's clothing. As Antichrist's high priest, he miraculously brings an image or statue of the beast to life, causing it to speak. His primary role is influencing every human being on planet Earth to worship the beast, even forcing them to if they refuse. He is also the instigator of the "mark of the beast," enforcing the law that every person receives the mark, without which they cannot buy or sell. Like the one he serves, he is both cunning and corrupt. And though inferior in power, this second beast is still just as ferocious.

"666"

The false prophet's role includes making sure every person receives "a mark on their right hand or on their forehead." *Everybody* gets the mark, regardless of race, nationality, or economic status. Without the mark, you're economically dead.[65] You can't buy food, pay a bill, or even purchase a pack of gum without it. Antichrist's economic chokehold on the world tightens significantly during the last three and a half years of the Great Tribulation.[66]

But there's more about this mark. The Greek word used here is *charagma*, a first-century term used to describe the image or names of emperors on Roman coins. The word was also used to indicate a stamp or seal on a document.[67] Whatever this mark is—an image, tattoo, implant, or some other representation—it's directly related to Antichrist himself and accomplishes two things:

1. It identifies a person as a worshipper of this satanic man.

2. It enables a person to engage in financial transactions.

The Rapture aftermath, along with the Third Seal Judgment, have made financial survival a near impossibility. Food is scarce and death is everywhere. The earth is not a happy place to live in, and the motivation to get your mark is very high. It will be the damning stamp of satanic slavery as there'll be no room for neutrality in the Tribulation.

And then John throws in this clue: "Here is wisdom. Let him who has understanding calculate the number of the beast, for the number is that of a man; and his number is six hundred and sixty-six."[68]

So what's the deal with 666, and what does it mean? As we've already learned, Antichrist's identity isn't revealed until after Christ comes to claim His bride. Further, ever since the second century, scribes and scholars have been trying to decipher the meaning of this cryptic number. John tells us 666 is the number of the beast, and is the number of a man.[69] He then suggests that the person "who has understanding calculate the number." That could reference a mathematical correlation using *gematria*, an ancient Jewish method used to find meanings in numbers. Each letter of the Hebrew alphabet carries a certain numerical equivalent. Converting someone's name into Hebrew, you can assign a number to that name. When applied to Antichrist, his numerical value is 666. The problem with *gematria* is that it's been used to assign the number of the beast to everyone from John Kennedy to Barak Obama.

I believe the "wisdom" and "understanding" referred to in Revelation 13:18 is meant for those who read Revelation during the Tribulation. The identity of Antichrist was seen as future in John's day just as it is in ours. Therefore, attempts to conclusively identify this beast today are futile and ridiculous. However, that does not mean Satan isn't currently grooming a man as a potential candidate should God begin setting the prophetic clock in motion. It also does not preclude certain contemporary individuals from exhibiting Antichrist-like characteristics and actions sympathetic with satanic values or an end-times agenda, such as hostility toward Christians and Jews and an international economic union.

It's also unclear whether this mark will simply make you eligible to buy and sell or will contain additional encoded information. There's no doubt that the technology for the "mark of the beast" is currently available. Radio Frequency Identification (RFID) technology has already been tested and approved by our own Food and Drug Administration. A little larger than a grain of rice, RFIDs have already been approved for medical use in monitoring and tracking patients and supplying medical information. It's even been considered for use by the Department of Homeland Security for identifying individuals at border checkpoints and for tracking purposes. Other technologies currently available include permanent, invisible RFID ink and epidermal electronic systems.[70]

No one knows exactly how this mark will work, other than what Scripture explicitly says. But what we can be sure of is that the technology is here right now and being used for other purposes.[71]

And though those who receive 666 may have, prior to the Rapture, associated it with evil, they will nevertheless willingly embrace it out of desperation while under the delusion of Antichrist's lies.[72] Scripture also makes it clear that not even one believer in Jesus will receive the mark, and that everyone who does will suffer God's wrath.[73]

There's so much more we could say about Satan's man of sin, some of which we'll address in the next chapter. But though he's become a centerpiece in the end-times narrative, in reality he's no more than a blip on God's radar. Leftover dust on the scales of history.[74] We don't know who he is, but we fear neither him nor the one who possesses him.[75] He and his master, Satan, are at the mercy of God's timetable and blueprint for history. That's because there's a sovereign "throne in heaven."[76]

Nevertheless, like a diligent warrior, the diabolical destroyer has been preparing for this hour for centuries. Author and prophecy expert Mark Hitchcock writes, "Satan does not know the exact time of Christ's return or when the restrainer will be removed, so he must have a potential candidate for the Antichrist ready in every generation."[77]

Again, we do not (and cannot) definitively know the identity of Antichrist until after the Rapture. Any claims to such knowledge should be dismissed by discerning believers. But the fact remains that Antichrist *is* coming. And he *could* be alive today.

Here's what we can be sure of—the world is not getting better. The current crumbling moral foundation of nations combined with growing international economic dependency is part of what's setting the stage for such a leader to arise. And the presence of the bride is the only thing currently holding back the man of sin. Her sudden Rapture rescue will set in motion his rise to prominence and power.

Antichrist is Satan's masterpiece. However, his authority is limited, otherwise he would continue his slaughter and reign indefinitely.[78]

It's now late in the Tribulation. Satan knows the clock is ticking and that his time is running out (12:12).

Meanwhile, in heaven, horses are being saddled.

10

Return Engagement!

While Antichrist rises to power during the final seven-year Tribulation, concurrent with his prominence will be a worldwide apostate religion known as "Babylon the great, the mother of harlots and of the abominations of the earth."[1]

The World's Oldest Profession

Babylon is an important location and a symbol of evil in Scripture,[2] and this religious system is personified here as a woman and called Babylon partially because she embodies the idolatrous religious system present in biblical history following Noah's flood.[3] It didn't take mankind long to run back into paganism following God's worldwide flood judgment, illustrating once again the inherent sinfulness of the human heart. Rejecting God's revealed truth, humanity once again began searching for significance and meaning in something other than their Creator. So they created their own religious system, which included building a city "and a tower whose top will reach into heaven."[4] They sought completeness without God, believing that divinity rested either naturally in themselves or was achievable through some human effort.

That same lie permeates the world today through human

philosophy and man-made religions. Through religious activity, rules, human "goodness," or enlightenment, man is still trying to reach the divine. This is one compelling reason why Christianity stands head and shoulders above every faith, philosophy, and religious system. We don't worry about reaching up to God because He already reached down to us. He did for us what we could never do for ourselves—make us righteous and whole.

So to quell this religious rebellion, God thwarted their tower-building efforts by confusing their language. No longer able to communicate, construction came to a halt, and God scattered them all over the world. To commemorate this event, they gave a name to the place where they attempted to build their religious monument, calling it Babel, from the Hebrew word meaning "to confuse."[5] From this point on, Babylon came to be associated with religious paganism and an evil empire.[6]

Now, in Revelation's prophecy, we see once again a resurgence of Babylonian prominence. Because John offers no literary signs pointing to this being merely a symbolic name, I believe a literal city of Babylon will be rebuilt on the banks of the Tigris-Euphrates Rivers.[7]

During the first three and a half years of the Tribulation, Babylon becomes the center of the world's new counterfeit religion. But what religion? Throughout church history, many have attempted to associate this great Babylonian prostitute with the Roman Catholic Church, noting such ecclesiastical similarities as opulent wealth, royal garments, and a history of persecuting believers. Religion and money have always made for a potent cocktail. Others see this religion as an apostate aberration of Christianity made up of what's left behind following the Rapture. Or it could be some pluralistic religious mash-up of spirituality and ancient paganism.

One thing is certain, though—there will be mass confusion following the Rapture as millions are snatched away. Because many of today's church-members are not truly born again, they, along with billions more, will be left behind, wondering what just happened.[8]

No doubt those religious leaders who remain will rally together, seeking to give hope and somehow explain this global phenomenon. They will have to rationalize this event in light of their ever-evolving theology, possibly leading to a "new understanding" of God and how to worship Him.[9] Whatever this new world religion is, it will be a monument to mankind's pride and self-righteous arrogance.

It's true today that Satan promotes pluralism, a relativistic approach to truth, and an evolving theology. However, the devil himself hasn't really changed since his fall. He himself cannot evolve, but merely adapts his age-old methods to fit the time, people, and circumstances. His character is eternally evil and his strategy remains the same—to deceive, lie, and counterfeit.[10] Having waited centuries, he now returns full circle, back to the place where he first instigated his unrighteous religion.

Portrayed as a fornicating prostitute, Babylon stands in stark contrast with the purity of Christ's bride. This religious system will vehemently persecute and kill those who believe in Jesus Christ. And yet the irony is that she herself will eventually be destroyed by Antichrist and his coalition of kings.[11]

So the Babylon of Revelation 17 refers to a worldwide apostate religious system engulfing the earth's population in the first half of the Tribulation.[12] It's also a literal city rebuilt to serve Satan's end-times strategy and used as Antichrist's political and economic headquarters.[13] John sees an angel with "great authority" describe political and economic Babylon as a "dwelling place of demons" whose "sins have piled up as high as heaven," perhaps another veiled reference to the tower of Babel.[14] But God pays her back "double according to her deeds." This wicked city will suddenly and catastrophically be destroyed by God in the Seventh Bowl Judgment.[15] Though religious and commercial Babylon indulges herself in the wine of immorality, greed, and even the blood of the saints, God prepares a drink especially mixed for her, fermented in His full fury and wrath.[16]

Armageddon

If you want to get someone's attention, just mention *Armageddon*. This word has become synonymous with apocalypse and the end of the world. It's a dark and weighty word. Interestingly, the word itself occurs only once in the entire Bible.[17] It comes from the Hebrew *Har* (mountain) and *Megiddo* (an ancient city built on a hill overlooking the Plain of Esdraelon, also known as the Valley of Jezreel). When people speak of Armageddon, they think of a battle, but it actually refers to a geographic location in Israel where a series of epic battles culminate.[18] This grand battlefield stretches out over twenty thousand square miles—two hundred miles north to south and one hundred miles east to west.

Revelation 16:12 tells us that the water of "the great river, the Euphrates" is "dried up," allowing "the kings from the east" to cross. This is already happening as the Euphrates water supply is drastically dwindling due to Turkey's water policies, turning wetlands into deserts.[19] These current conditions help set the stage for future prophetic fulfillment.

Following this, three demonic spirits emanating from the phony trinity of Satan, the beast, and the false prophet gather the armies of the entire world together for a climactic battle, even performing supernatural signs to lure and persuade them to assemble for war.[20] It's not clear what the initial motivation for this battle is. It could be a call to annihilate Israel once and for all, as according to Old Testament prophecy, Jerusalem will be attacked at this time, her houses plundered, and her women raped.[21] This vendetta against Israel is as old as the nation itself. Adding to this hatred, Israel's God has brought all this judgment and destruction on planet Earth. So what better scapegoat than the Jews?

The world has a long history of hatred for this race and the chosen covenant nation through which the Messiah would come. Now, at last, Satan concludes, the Hebrews can be exterminated once and for all time. What Hitler began with his "final solution" campaign can now be realized.[22]

Ironic that the earth's mightiest empires have ultimately proved impotent against this peculiar little nation and race. Egypt kept them as slaves and suffered horrific plagues as a result. Babylon, Assyria, and Persia conquered and captured them, and those nations now lie on the ash heap of history. Rome subjugated and persecuted the Jews, ultimately scattering them to the wind. Today, the words *Roman* and *ruins* are inseparably linked. In more recent history, Germany led a genocidal campaign to rid Europe of the *Judenschwein* (Jewpig). That country was brought to its knees in WWII, afterward becoming a divided nation.

This brings to mind the unchanging promise of God to Abraham concerning the nation that would come from him,

> "And I will bless those who bless you,
> And the one who curses you I will curse.
> And in you all the families of the earth will be
> blessed."[23]

God's unconditional promises never go unfulfilled. And though Israel as a nation has been placed on the back burner until the "fullness of the Gentiles has come in," He has not forgotten her.[24]

And so, armies of the world, made up of tens of millions, perhaps more, gather together at Armageddon. They are locked and loaded and lusting for blood. But they are in for an apocalyptic surprise.

The Galloping Christ

While it is impossible to know what will be in the hearts and minds of those untold millions of soldiers gathered at Armageddon, it's safe to assume they are prepared to wage war. A worldwide hatred of God, fueled by Satan and self, has filtered down to each individual (or filtered up *from* them). We do know that by this point in the

Tribulation, men are cursing and blaspheming God with stubborn, unrepentant hatred.[25]

However, at some point in this battle campaign, perhaps even before a single shot is fired, something unexpected happens. A moment arrives, predestined in eternity past, when every eye on that vast battlefield suddenly turns its gaze upward. Bursting through the clouds is a sight no mortal man has ever beheld.[26] It's not the manger Christ Child but the Majestic Messiah. He's not humbly seated upon a lowly donkey, but galloping victoriously upon a white warhorse, a stark contrast to the comparative impotence of Antichrist as rider.[27] The prophetic promise announced at Jesus's ascension[28] has finally come to pass. And nobody saw Him coming, as He had previously warned He would come as a thief in the night—unannounced, uninvited, and unwelcome.[29]

Revelation 19:11 gives us a name for this rider. He is called "Faithful and True." He is the same "faithful witness" of Revelation 1:5 who has unveiled this entire Revelation message to the bride through John. He is also called here "the Word of God," the perfect incarnation and expression of the invisible God.[30] He is the true Christ, replacing the counterfeit, wannabe messiah the world is accustomed to seeing. John then announces the two specific reasons for Jesus's sudden, unexpected appearance.

1. To judge.
2. To make war.[31]

This is the Jesus a sleeping bride knows little about. We're very familiar with the Savior who loves, leads, and carries our burdens. We have a fond affection for the Christ who answers our prayers. We can quote John 3:16 backward. We wear His cross around our necks and sometimes open His Bible. And we love the part about Jesus being a friend to sinners. However, we have yet to become acquainted with the Son of God who *judges* sinners. We don't usually talk about *that* Jesus because we prefer to keep things positive. Besides, we're afraid people won't like our Jesus if we tell them He's coming to judge them unless they repent.[32] That's not considered "effective evangelism."

But Jesus is both the lover of sinners and the judge of them. With God, there are times and even ages where grace and mercy are freely offered. That's because He's a gracious and merciful Lord. But there are also times when judgment and wrath prevail. That's because He's a judgmental and wrathful Lord. God is not one-dimensional. He is as righteous and wrathful as He is loving, as vengeful as He is kind. And there is exactly zero contradiction between those attributes. No conflict between them whatsoever. They are not diametrically opposed character qualities, but rather blend together in supernatural, incomprehensible harmony. And so, yes, God has friends *and* enemies.[33] Calvary was a place and time of sacrifice. The garden tomb a place and time of triumph. And Armageddon will be a place and time of righteous and brutal execution.

At the Rapture, Christ comes in the air. At the Second Coming, He lands on earth. The Rapture brought rejoicing and reunion. The Second Coming brings retribution.

Perhaps with wide-eyed amazement, John continues putting pen to parchment and records what he sees. He notes that this conquering warrior and judge has fiery penetrating eyes. Second-Coming Jesus sees the condition of every heart gathered for battle. He is crowned with many crowns, signifying both His inherent and earned right to rule. He has a name written upon Him that no one knows but Himself.[34] John sees this name, but it is indecipherable to him. This mystery may have special meaning for this event, or it may relate somehow to the "new name" He promised to those who overcome.[35] This galloping Christ wears a bloodstained robe, perhaps prefiguring the blood He is about to spill.[36] His eyes, crowns, and robe are visible to the whole earth either through technology or supernaturally made possible by the glory of His exalted presence.

In a scene that is simultaneously gory and glorious, Jesus's visible descent from the sky foreshadows to earth's armies the horror that awaits them, igniting a deep dread within.[37]

In the age of grace, an "acceptable time" of salvation was offered and available.[38] And yet here, much like Noah's ark of salvation, God Himself has slammed shut that door of opportunity.[39] Those alive during the Tribulation will no doubt, like many today, mock the promise of Christ's return, dismissing it as a faith-based fairy tale. But at the Valley of Megiddo, it has become reality. God's patience has run its course and His plan for history and humanity moves forward.[40]

John's vision is officially about to go brutal here as Scripture describes, in graphic detail, Jesus's terrible and righteous judgment. Oh, how fearless and authentic God's Word is, never holding back, especially when the truth gets uncomfortable. The Bible is certainly not a book for the faint of heart.

Reading about Jesus's Second Coming is meant to evoke a tangible response in His bride, leading her to repentance, reverence, rejoicing, or shock and silence. However, it cannot leave her unaffected. If this section of Scripture doesn't stir the church from her slumber, we may need to check for a pulse. Besides, all Christ followers should naturally connect with this scene because we will be a part of it! We are galloping behind Jesus on this ride into battle. Revelation 19:14 states, "And the armies which are in heaven, clothed in fine linen, white and clean, were following Him on white horses."

The coming Christ is accompanied by a great army, bursting through the clouds and riding in formation on heavenly horses. We are that bride from heaven, clothed in "fine linen, bright and clean," representing our righteous acts.[41] Earlier, this same group is referred to as "the called and chosen and faithful."[42] Joining us in this huge formation of riders are those who have suffered and died during the Tribulation.[43] And according to Jesus, mighty angels will also flank Him in this mission.[44]

There is no reason to take the presence of horses here as anything other than actual, literal creatures. In Scripture, horses represent military strength, and here they are charging into battle by the tens of millions.

Mere words and human emotion are insufficient to describe what we will be feeling on that day. But this we do know. Unlike past military heroes who have stormed beaches or ridden furiously into the face of the enemy, there will be no apprehension or fear for us. Descending from the sky that day, our fright will have long been replaced by confidence and holy zeal.

Touch Down!

Scripture says we are "following Him."[45] No doubt called to formation in heaven, we will all gladly mount up and line up behind our Savior and King. Think of the freedom to obey Him then considering our struggle to follow during our earthly lives. Jesus originally called His disciples with a simple "follow Me."[46] All during our lives, He issued the same daily invitation to His bride as the secret to her joy.[47] Now again, He commands us to follow Him into battle, judgment, and victory. What a divine privilege. What a holy honor to follow the Captain of the Lord's army into battle![48]

The prophet Zechariah, looking forward many centuries to this event, faithfully records, "On that day his feet will stand on the Mount of Olives, east of Jerusalem, and the Mount of Olives will be split in two from east to west, forming a great valley, with half of the mountain moving north and half moving south."[49]

Before engaging His enemies, Jesus returns to the very Mount of Olives He had ascended from, exactly as the angels predicted in Acts 1:11.[50] His feet touch Jewish soil, perhaps at the precise spot where in Matthew 24:3 He spoke of these end-times events. Or He could touch down at the spot from which His disciples witnessed His being caught up (raptured) to heaven. Whatever the case, He lands with authority, causing a massive, violent earthquake that splits the

Mount of Olives north and south. It's more than a coincidence that recent geological surveys have revealed this area to be at imminent risk for major earthquake activity.[51]

But wait, this whole Second Coming scenario may sound a bit over the top for some Christians. To those whose personalities tend to be nonconfrontational or timid, this may seem traumatic. After all, isn't Christianity a peaceful faith? You may even wonder, "What if I don't like violence? Do I still have to go?"

First, don't panic. To begin with, consider that even this side of heaven, some wars and military campaigns are justified in order to preserve human freedom and prevent the subjugation of peace-loving people. If there were no injustice or evil, there would be no reason for war.

Second, this event flows from the heart of a holy and perfect God. Jesus's return is not a terrorist attack on an innocent population, but a righteous retribution upon an evil, blaspheming planet. And as the angel of the Third Bowl Judgment earlier stated, "They deserve it." In our culture that calls evil good and good evil, we may sometimes forget that there are bad people who do horrible things and deserve to be arrested and removed from society. We forget that man is not basically good but inherently evil.[52]

Third, at the Rapture or death, your sin nature is totally eradicated. By this time, your mind will be radically changed and made like Christ's.[53] You'll see as He sees and understand all things from God's perspective. And you will fully comprehend and embrace God's righteous justice against the wicked.

Fourth, the Lord returns to slay His enemies quickly. Even so, their eternal punishment soon follows their swift death.

Finally, Jesus is the only one who is said to possess a weapon in this battle. Though we are called the "armies which are in heaven," we carry no weapons of warfare.[54] We are warriors, but our conquering King does all the fighting. And His weapon of choice? A sword: "From His mouth comes a sharp sword, so that with it He may strike down the nations, and He will rule them with a rod of iron; and He treads the wine press of the fierce wrath of God, the Almighty."[55]

The sword Jesus wields in this battle is not held in His hand but flows from His mouth. The glorified Christ doesn't require a physical weapon. His Word is all the power He needs. By His Word the heavens and earth were formed.[56] With only a word from His mouth He healed the sick, raised the dead, calmed the storm, cursed a fig tree, and shut demons' mouths, casting them out. His Word, whether spoken or written, is a double-edged sword.[57] Since His departure from earth, His bride is to have been nourished on this Word, drinking it like milk and eating it like meat.[58] His powerful Word is our source of truth and the bedrock upon which we build our lives, relationships, marriages, families, and the church.[59] It is our offensive weapon against the enemy, the devil and his "spiritual forces of wickedness."[60] And it is everything the bride needs for life and godliness.[61]

That same Word, impossible to separate from the person of Christ Himself, will "strike down the nations." Staring into those flaming eyes, those at Armageddon will have no chance to launch a counterattack. In this, the ultimate battlefield "shock and awe," not a trigger will likely be pulled nor a shot fired. Instead, they will all be annihilated, crushed like grapes in a winepress.[62]

It will be a slaughter so great that their blood will flow in some places four and a half feet high for a distance of two hundred miles![63] This is why John describes this carnage as the "fierce wrath of God, the Almighty."[64] With that in mind, read what the author of Hebrews says to those who are exposed to God's truth but who nonchalantly brush it off and reject it.

> For if we go on sinning willfully after receiving the knowledge of the truth, there no longer remains a sacrifice for sins, but a terrifying expectation of judgment and the fury of a fire which will consume the adversaries.

> Anyone who has set aside the Law of Moses dies with-
> out mercy on the testimony of two or three witnesses.
> How much severer punishment do you think he will
> deserve who has trampled under foot the Son of God,
> and has regarded as unclean the blood of the covenant
> by which he was sanctified, and has insulted the Spirit of
> grace? For we know Him who said, "Vengeance is Mine,
> I will repay." And again, "The Lord will judge His peo-
> ple." It is a terrifying thing to fall into the hands of the
> living God.[65]

Those who today trample the Son of God with their apathy,
pride, stubbornness, and unbelief will themselves one day be tram-
pled by His wrath. Believing in Jesus is not some cafeteria option
that's available just in case you need it. Just in case Christianity fits
your idea of religion or life. No, as Paul stated, God "commands all
people everywhere to repent."[66] Salvation in Christ is much more
than a kind offer; it's a requirement that brings life and eternity's best
to us. This gracious God has given mankind the gift of choice, but
those foolish enough to reject His love will live with eternal regret.

Though it may originally have been unclear why the world's military forces gathered in this place for battle, eventually their ultimate purpose is revealed. John says "the kings of the earth and their
armies assembled to make war against Him who sat on the horse
and against His army."[67] Earth goes to war against Jesus, and the
risen, glorified Christ prevails.

Finally, John tells us one more thing he notices about this Righteous Rider from the sky. On His robe and thigh (perhaps a banner)
is a name written, "King of kings and Lord of lords."[68]

Proclaiming the grandeur and greatness of Christ is a theme
repeated throughout Revelation. But it's not as though Jesus Himself needs the reminder or the attention. No, this displayed name is
a pregame proclamation of judgment and victory. As believers, we

need to remind ourselves often of His majesty and right to reign. This Revelation chorus of Christ's greatness is meant for us to dwell on and draw strength from its grand truth. It's a one-of-a-kind designation, reserved for Jesus alone. It announces to unbelievers the futility of allegiance to earthly kings over loyalty to the One True King. His title is the ultimate smackdown to Satan, Antichrist, and the false prophet for their bogus claims to deity and royalty.

This regal name is a universal declaration of His preeminence and dominance over all men, especially those who claim authority, position, or power. On that day, all earthly kings and lords, including generals, commanders, and mighty men, will suffer the same fate as corporals and privates. They will all be utterly decimated "with the sword which came from the mouth of Him who sat on the horse."[69] Immediately following this, an angel supernaturally summons "all the birds" of the air to come and feast and fill their stomachs on their corpses.[70]

The beast and his false prophet are then seized and "thrown alive into the lake of fire which burns with brimstone."[71]

Jesus Christ has returned!

11

Heaven *Is* for Real, But You Haven't Been There... Yet

There's a lot of misinformation floating around about heaven these days. In an age of renewed interest in the afterlife, there's no shortage of speculations and unbelievable stories regarding the hereafter. Of course, every religion or philosophy has some belief about what happens to you when you pass on—everything ranging from reincarnation to nirvana to annihilation. Christianity is no exception. But unlike all other faiths and belief systems, Jesus actually validated His claims about eternal life by rising from the grave and conquering death.

My Little Pony?

That hasn't stopped some in Christian circles from launching into their own authoritative-sounding tales of the great beyond. One best-selling book recounts the supposed experience of a four-year-old boy who, while under anesthesia, claims to have traveled to heaven. Once there, he received his own halo and angel wings (which he said were too small for his liking). He says Mary was standing beside Jesus's throne and that the Holy Spirit was bluish in color. He also claims Jesus was riding a rainbow-colored horse.

I know what you're thinking. *No intelligent Christian would actually believe such nonsense, right?* Wrong. Millions have swallowed this story, duped by what, in reality, sounds like an anesthesia-induced dream. I'm surprised he didn't claim to have met the Tin Man and Scarecrow too. A simple survey of Scripture reveals nothing about angel wings on believers. No halos. No blue Holy Spirit and no Jesus riding a rainbow pony.

Another boy, paralyzed in a car accident, also claims to have gone to heaven while in a coma. He also wrote a best-selling book, claiming that in heaven he saw not only Jesus but also the devil, who had "moldy teeth." Years later, the now teenage boy says, "I made it up because I thought it would get me attention."[1]

It did.

What a sad commentary on the bride of Christ that she would be so easily deceived by unbiblical claims of heavenly visits by little boys.[2] These are the kinds of things the apostle Paul was afraid would happen to Jesus's bride.[3]

We live in a time when many Christians are "tossed here and there by waves and carried about by every wind of doctrine."[4] The reason for this is that they're not grounded in the truth. If a certain story becomes popular among millions of Christians, then it must be true, right? Ours is also an age where God, morality, and truth are often determined and understood according to individual preference. As a result of this spirit of relativity and personal autonomy, many sincere Christians have unknowingly been pressed into the mold of worldly thinking.

The message that emerges from this biblical illiteracy and theological bankruptcy becomes: "Doctrine, morality, and heaven are *whatever you want them to be.*" It's as if God is saying, "Would you like your Jesus with blue eyes? Done. What about a tricked out, customized halo? Or a field of dreams baseball experience? We can make it happen, because here in heaven, we aim to please. Customer satisfaction is our number one priority."

Is this biblical Christianity or some twisted, misguided fantasy of human imagination? Again, how can you really know if someone saw the devil walking around heaven with moldy teeth? Because those making such assertions may be sincere, nice people, how can their claims be verified?

They can't.

Remember, we live in a culture where merely saying or believing something somehow carries with it inherent validation. It becomes rude to question someone's experience, even though God tells us to question our beliefs and experiences to make sure they line up with Scripture. [5]

Some may argue, "What's the big deal? If some kid wants to imagine Jesus on a rainbow horse, what harm is there in that?"

To begin with, there is a difference between a harmless child's dream and encouraging that child to invent his own truth about God, Jesus, the Holy Spirit, and heaven. Can you think of a more dangerous heresy than that? If we cannot trust the Bible concerning heaven, how can we trust it when it speaks of other truths about God, Jesus, salvation, hell, sexuality, and relationships?

I once heard a Christian remark, "If it's important to you, it will be in heaven."

Really? There are lots of important things in life that I am pretty sure won't be in heaven. Is the next life nothing more than a souped-up mental projection of personal preferences from this life? Are we to think of heaven like ordering up a drive-thru cheeseburger?

And we wonder why the world mocks Christians, refusing to take us seriously.

To date, dozens of books have been written about supposed trips to heaven, all claiming to be legitimate. And yet they contradict one another in their accounts of what heaven is like. This alone should cause us to be skeptical of their claims. Not to mention the fact that they don't square with Scripture's account of what heaven is like!

But no matter how cute, mushy, fantastic, childlike, or innocent someone's claim may be, getting authoritative information about heaven from any source other than God's Word is to enter a fairy tale. At worst, it's heresy that grossly misleads Jesus's bride. Stories like these should be summarily rejected in view of what God actually has revealed to us about heaven. Besides, who would choose to believe fabricated stories over God's inspired, inerrant Word? I mean, who does that?

A sleeping bride, that's who.

Phil Johnson writes,

> Only four authors in all the Bible were blessed with visions of heaven and wrote about what they saw: the prophets Isaiah and Ezekiel, and the apostles Paul and John. Two other biblical figures—Micaiah and Stephen—got glimpses of heaven, but what they saw is merely mentioned, not described (2 Chronicles 18:18; Acts 7:55). As Pastor [John] MacArthur points out, all of these were prophetic *visions*, not near-death experiences. Not one person raised from the dead in the Old or New Testaments ever recorded for us what he or she experienced in heaven. That includes Lazarus, who spent four days in the grave.
>
> Paul was caught up into heaven in an experience so vivid he said he didn't know whether he went there bodily or not, but he saw things that are unlawful to utter, so he gave no details. He covered the whole incident in just three verses (2 Corinthians 12:2-4).
>
> All three biblical writers who saw heaven and described their visions give comparatively sparse details, but they agree perfectly (Isaiah 6:1-4; Ezekiel 1 and 10; Revelation 4–6)… The biblical authors are all fixated on God's glory, which defines heaven and illuminates everything there.

They are overwhelmed, chagrined, petrified, and put to silence by the sheer majesty of God's holiness. Notably missing from all the biblical accounts are the frivolous features and juvenile attractions that seem to dominate every account of heaven currently on the bestseller lists.[6]

So Paul was forbidden to talk about his heavenly experience and, while there, heard words that were "inexpressible," which he was not allowed to repeat. What he saw and heard was so wonderful that he was given a "thorn in the flesh" to keep him humble about his experience.[7] And what did others with death experiences say about heaven?

Lazarus. Nothing recorded (John 11:44).

Widow of Nain's son. Zero words mentioned (Luke 7:14).

Tabitha. Nada (Acts 9).

Eutychus. Zilch (Acts 20).

Learning to Discern

At some point, every growing Christian must ask, "Do I really trust the Bible? Is God's Word enough to fulfill my wonder and curiosity about heaven? Or do I need fantasy and false narrative to fill in the blanks?" If you answer yes to that final question, heaven could end up being a huge disappointment for you.

But there are other valid reasons these supposed visits to heaven cannot be trusted:

- They can't be verified as it is impossible to substantiate such claims. Such "out of body experiences" are purely subjective and more common in pagan traditions than in biblical Christianity.

- If they were true, they become *new revelation* about God and the afterlife and should be added to Scripture, even though God specifically forbids doing this.[8]

- God has already declared how He feels about false prophets, warning us to not "believe every spirit" but to "test the spirits" with truth and discernment, and to "examine yourselves to see whether you are in the faith."[9]

- Satan regularly disguises himself as an angel of light, mixing a tasty, intoxicating drink of truth and lies through human deceit and false teaching.[10] And yet, it still sounds somehow cruel and unkind to reject the story of a cute, innocent boy who says he died and went to heaven, right? How dare we?

- Many young Christians today are biblically illiterate and therefore doctrinally deficient, with no filter through which to discern such claims other than their own feelings. As a result, they fall for just about anything, and just as Paul predicted, are tossed back and forth by every wind of doctrine. A part of growing into maturity is not falling for these false narratives.[11]

- Paul also prophesied that in the last days, men would fall away from the faith, paying attention to seducing spirits and doctrines of demons.[12]

Imagine the following conversation:

Christian: "But these ideas about heaven sound so sweet, God."

God: "Yes, I know. But they're not true. Doesn't that matter to you?"

Christian: "Well, they *might* be true. And besides, I just wish You had told us more about heaven. I mean, I have so many questions."

God: "My child, do you really want to start inventing ideas about Me? That's what I call idolatry, and I already showed you how I feel about that in My Word. Remember Exodus 20 and that golden calf episode? You can't simply conjure up authoritative ideas about My Son, My character, salvation, heaven or hell—mainly because your ideas won't do Me justice. I love you more than that. That's why I gave you My revelation, so you could have *My* thoughts on all these things. Your thoughts about heaven are incomplete and not worthy of Me.[13] Instead, trust My Word, and I promise that heaven will be much better than what anyone has claimed or described."

In a Christian culture that often equates success, numbers, and money with God's blessing and validation, we think, *If it sells, it must be a God thing.* Scripture makes no such correlation or value assessment.

Good and sincere people can be deceived, even by their own hearts and imaginations. But after two thousand years of growth, maturity, and access to the Word of God, many Christians still opt for fables over God's written revelation. This not only speaks to our lack of biblical grounding and spiritual discernment, but also insults the reality of heaven itself. Why pay attention to caricatures of heaven when we can get actual, accurate descriptions from God Himself? Why settle for fairy tales when the real thing is printed right in front of us in black and white?

These claims scream, "I know more than the Bible!" That's not only unintelligent, it's heretical. This isn't about attacking other believers or playing Holy Spirit. It's just that when such falsehood is embraced by millions, it should be denounced and then dumped in the trash as heresy.

I realize these are harsh words, but I write them intentionally. The purity of Jesus's bride cannot be taken lightly. She is preparing herself for her groom, and as Paul feared, her innocence and devotion to Him must be carefully guarded, lest she be deceived.[14] Our truth comes from Scripture, not people's dreams, drug-induced hallucinations, or supposed trips to the afterlife.

I believe part of our struggle is that many in the church have been taught to prefer syrupy spirituality over pure doctrine. In our immaturity and longing for tangible evidence for our faith, we choose emotion over revelation because one makes us feel good and the other requires faith and submitting our beliefs to God's. That's how crippled we've become in our fallen humanity. In our weakness, we can embrace teaching simply because it makes us feel good, comforting us and validating our wishes or ideas. I've been guilty of this as well. But the truth is that there's still plenty to get emotional about when it comes to the Bible's description of heaven.

So, instead of putting our trust in stories and questionable experiences, why not read what God has already written on the subject of heaven?

Yes, heaven *is* for real. But our dreams are not.

A Sneak Preview of the Afterlife

The writer of Revelation (who *was* allowed to tell about his vision of heaven) was also commissioned to write it down as divine revelation for the church and for it to be included in the canon of Scripture. So what does the Bible say about heaven? What do we know for sure?

Returning to Revelation, the Tribulation has passed. Jesus has come back and Armageddon is over. Following this, Satan is bound as Christ reigns on earth for a thousand years.[15] I believe this is a literal one thousand years.[16] During this time, we will celebrate the marriage supper of the Lamb, reign with Christ, oversee cities, judge angels, and even govern nations.[17]

At the end of this thousand years, Satan is released and is allowed to incite a final rebellion against God among the nations.[18] This uprising and revolt will be quickly foiled by fire from the sky. Following this, Satan is thrown into the lake of fire where he, the beast, and the false prophet burn forever.[19]

The great white throne judgment is next. Those who've died without Christ all throughout history are brought before His throne to be judged by Him "from whose presence earth and heaven fled

away" (20:11). This includes everyone—kings and peasants, rich
and poor, old and young, famous and insignificant, evil murders
and law-abiding citizens—from every religion and from no religion.
Anyone whose name is not found in the book of life is thrown into
the lake of fire. [20] How tragic is the destiny of those who choose self
and sin over a Savior who loves them.

Now comes the eternal state or heaven. And just to calm any fears
you may have, heaven will also not be one big, very long church service. We won't sit in pews or chairs while people speak or sing on
stage for eternity.

So what *do* we know about heaven? What are the undeniable
facts? On Jesus's last night with His disciples, He revealed several
important things about the heaven that awaits His bride. Here's
what we learn from Jesus's words in John 14:1-3.

Heaven is a real place. Jesus referred to heaven as "My Father's
house." It's not a psychological state of mind, philosophical concept,
or happy thought. It's not some warm feeling Jesus conjured up to
comfort us. Rather, it's a literal, physical place, as real as the chair
you're sitting in. It's a place you can see, feel, touch, and experience.
Heaven *exists*. Aren't you glad?

Heaven is a prepared place. Think of it! Jesus Himself, the Savior and author of creation and creativity, is designing a place *for you.*

Heaven is a place of fulfilled promises. Consider the context of
Christ's words. He's speaking on what would prove to be His last
night with His best friends. He would soon die, leaving them and
returning to the Father. The separation would be painful. But He
promises to return and take His followers to heaven one day. That
promise will begin its fulfillment at the Rapture.

Heaven is the place where God is. More than anything, heaven is
where Jesus dwells, and we get to be with Him there. The primary
reason Jesus chose His disciples is that they might "be with Him." [21]
It's the reason He's returning for them. [22] It's one of the last requests

He asked of the Father just before being arrested, tortured, and crucified.[23] Even heaven itself is described this way: "the tabernacle of God is among men, and He will dwell among them, and they shall be His people, and God Himself will be among them."[24]

But imagine for a moment that this was the only thing we knew about heaven—that God is there and that we'll be with Him.

Would that be enough for you?

If you took everything you knew and have experienced with God thus far and simply multiplied it in length and strength, would that be heaven enough for you? What you long for heaven to be reveals what you love and desire most about God. So is the promise of God's person and presence enough to produce a deep longing and anticipation of heaven for you?

Because an infinitely wise, loving, and creative God is preparing heaven for us, it cannot fully be described with human language, art, music, drama, or earthly comparisons. There simply aren't enough superlatives, though God *has* given us glimpses of this future glory. He knows if we really understood how great heaven is going to be, we would be tempted to abandon our mission here and immediately go there. After all, to be with Christ is "very much better."[25] It's indescribable, incomprehensible, and unimaginable.

Heaven and Earth: Extreme Makeover Edition

After the present heaven and earth are destroyed following the millennium, God will create a "new heaven and a new earth."[26] This is what Paul spoke of, what Abraham looked for, and what every believer seeks.[27] This new heaven and earth is the eternal state, and is also described as the "bride, the wife of the Lamb," possibly because we will identify with it as our eternal home.[28] The main attraction in this "new heaven" is God Himself. He is there. With us. Eternally. This truth speaks of the incredible intimate relationship we'll have with our Lord. The fulfillment we receive from all human relationships here on earth will be eclipsed by the overwhelming satisfaction of what we'll have with Him then. He will be our God and we will be His children.[29]

Heaven *is* being with God.

However, this same God also wants us to know what *won't* be in heaven. We discover that things found in abundance down here will long be extinct in our eternal dwelling place. For example, there will be:

No sea (21:1)—John had described the sea as being "the source of the satanic beast (13:1) and the place of the dead (20:13)."[30] So no devil or demons.

No tears (21:4)—because they're wiped away by God Himself. He's that near to us!

No death (21:4)—as previously witnessed in earth and in the millennial kingdom.[31]

No mourning (21:4)—because the grief associated with death, sin, or suffering is gone forever.

No crying (21:4)—because there's no emotional trauma or stress leading to tears. Our happiness will never again be threatened.

No pain (21:4)—because nothing exists to harm us physically.

No thirst (21:6; 22:1)—because the crystal clear water of life is ours to drink at will.

No wickedness (21:8,27)—because sin is gone. And sinners cannot cross the threshold of heaven, being confined forever to the lake of fire.[32]

No temple (21:22)—because God is the temple, and we dwell with Him.

No night (21:23-25; 22:5)—because the glory of God illumines all of heaven.

No closed gates (21:25)—because we have eternal access, and there's no threat of attack.

No curse (22:3)—because the downward heart-pull of sin is no more. No one struggles with temptation. The inner zombie (sin nature) is nonexistent. We're free at last!

But there's even more He's revealed to us about our eternal home. Heaven is also a place where:

1. Earthly pursuits and sufferings will seem trivial in light of the new understanding and transformation we'll experience.[33]

2. Colors, music, aromas, knowledge, enjoyment, laughter, happiness, satisfaction, and pleasure are all heightened in a way we've never known.[34] In a re-created heaven and earth, Jesus makes all things new![35] Perhaps this is why C.S. Lewis wrote, "Joy is the serious business of heaven."[36]

3. Races are reconciled and all relationships are made perfect.

4. Our bodies are transformed, made like Christ's resurrection body.[37] Therefore, we may share some or all of His physical characteristics:

   • Physically glorified—not floating spirits[38]

   • Never sick, tired, hurt, or diseased[39]

   • Supernaturally equipped bodies, transformed to withstand the intensity of heaven's glory and the presence of Almighty God[40]

   • Able to pass through physical objects[41]

   • Perhaps able to transport ourselves or instantly appear or disappear[42]

   • Able to talk, eat, and drink.[43] In fact, Jesus promised He would eat and drink with us at our wedding feast.

So you see, the Bible actually tells us quite a bit about our heavenly home, the "New Jerusalem." We will have something there we never had during our earthly lives, namely clarity and completeness.

The Celestial Cube

John's vision of the New Jerusalem is unique, to say the least. He sees this heavenly city measuring 1500 miles high, deep, and wide—a perfect cube. Mark Hitchcock pictures it for us this way,

> To help us envision it, we can think of a map of the United States. The footprint of the city would be about the same as drawing a square from Miami up to Maine then westward to Minneapolis then south to Houston and then back to Miami. And that's just the ground level. The towering city rises 1500 miles.[44]

This celestial city-cube floats above the earth, one day coming to rest upon it.[45] Admittedly, this concept is difficult to visualize. Nevertheless, it is what it is. So let's explore it further.[46] This massive dwelling place will be lit by the glory of God shining in it. Its walls are 1500 miles long and 216 feet thick, and are composed of jasper, possibly transparent or diamond-like. There are twelve gates to this city, three each on the east, north, south, and west. Each gate is made from a single pearl and the names of the twelve tribes of Israel are inscribed on each gate. Twelve angels are stationed at these gates, which are never closed.

This city has twelve foundation stones on which are the names of the twelve apostles. Each foundation stone is a different precious stone. Interesting that the gates and the foundations of this city represent both Israel and the church, indicative of the two groups being perpetually distinct and yet united through Christ in heaven.

There is one street mentioned in this city, and it's made of pure, transparent gold. Again, there's no temple or sun or night, as God Himself is the light we see and walk by. There's no need for security or police as no evildoers live in this city. Instead, only those whose names are written in the Lamb's book of life reside here.

A "river of the water of life," coming from the throne of God and of the Lamb, flows through the middle of the street. This water tastes like eternal life, and it is flanked by the "tree of life" which bears twelve kinds of fruit each month. This is the tree Adam and Eve were excluded from in the Garden following their sin. But in the New Jerusalem, there will be no restrictions on it or on us. I believe this is the place Jesus was ultimately referring to in John 14:1-3. This is His Father's house. All told, the New Jerusalem is 3.375 billion cubic miles of pure heaven.[47]

There's No Place like Home

For the bride, there is something about heaven that mystically draws her, something in every reborn heart that longs for a place like this. I think God put that desire within us. The desire for *home*. A place where we *belong*.

But have you ever wondered what we will do for eternity? Despite what you may have wondered or been led to believe, heaven will never be boring. Boredom is a product of fallen humanity. It's something we currently experience when we find our minds and spirits disengaged and unstimulated. When bored, we long for something more, something else...anything! But in heaven, we'll experience a perfect balance and fulfillment of activity, mental stimulation, and spiritual and emotional satisfaction. So being bored is logically impossible in heaven. We conceive of heaven being boring only because we've been misinformed and because our finite minds can't yet grasp the future fulfillment we'll know there.

Since God is the originator of all fun and enjoyment, you can be sure nobody will be yawning in heaven. We're not told all of what we'll do, but we do know:

- We'll serve Christ in amazing ways He has yet to reveal to us.[48]

- We'll experience with one another the greatest level of friendship and fellowship possible.[49]

- We'll rest.[50]
- And we'll engage in a never-ending joyous adventure as we discover and experience more about God, His universe, and our salvation.

But that's not all. Keep in mind that all our senses will be heightened to their ultimate capacity and fulfillment.

Tell Me More!

Not long ago, while visiting my parents in South Carolina, my eighty-seven-year-old dad asked, "Jeff, will we know each other in heaven?"

Having only recently called on the Lord for salvation, he had begun wondering about heaven and if he would ever see his dear mother and father again.

"Yes, Dad," I confidently replied. "We will definitely know each other in heaven." Looking up at the black-and-white photographs of my grandparents on the wall, I assured him, "You will see Granny and Papa Kinley again."

And the tears rolled down his cheeks.

Someone once asked legendary pastor W.A. Criswell the same question. He replied, "Yes. In fact, we won't really know each other *until* we get to heaven."

Our current capacity for relationships is hindered because of sin, immaturity, insecurity, and poor people skills. But all these will be perfected in our eternal home. Yes, we will definitely know each other. Peter recognized Moses and Elijah when they came down from heaven for a short visit, and Jesus indicated we'll all retain our individual identities in heaven.[51] I believe we'll immediately know everyone in the afterlife, including not only friends and family who have gone before us, but also all the great saints of the Bible and throughout history. Won't it be great to ask Noah about his ark experience? Or Elijah about his chariot ride? Or Moses about parting the

Red Sea? There will be endless reunions, experiences, and exhilarating discussions in heaven.

Others wonder whether we will be married in heaven. We won't be, but this is good news. Marriage as we know it is an earthly relationship and one that will pass away.[52] In heaven, those who were married on earth experience a deeper and more fulfilling connection with their former spouses. Glorified in Him, we'll *finally* have a perfect relationship with our earthly mate. But even better is that we, as Christ's bride, will participate in another special wedding event.

God the Father, having chosen His Son's bride in eternity past, and betrothed her to Him during her time on earth, inaugurates the marriage ceremony in heaven following the Rapture and the judgment seat of Christ.[53] After this, the party begins, as we participate in the "marriage supper of the Lamb."[54] This celebration will be like none other, and could last for the entire one thousand year reign of Christ on earth![55]

What else will not be in heaven? Lots of stuff. Things we'll never see or experience again include sin, suffering, death, grief, mental-health issues, pain, cancer, addiction, AIDS, abuse, murder, abortion, divorce, disabilities, racial prejudice, stress, war, persecution, fighting, hurt feelings, disappointment, worry, emptiness, or any unmet need.[56] Sound good so far?

In addition, worship in heaven won't be like worship here on earth. We can experience true worship here, but just not like in heaven. There won't be any bands on a stage with concert lighting, synchronized hand-raising, and lyrics projected on a big screen. In heaven, it's worship of another kind. Worship from another dimension and in a different language. Worship on a totally different level and scale. Worship that transcends our current understanding and capacity. It's a complete surrender of our spirits to the One who is worthy. We'll be unhindered and motivated from within to declare His grandeur and worth through praise. And God apparently likes His worship loud.[57]

Heaven draws us homeward for so many reasons. It's the ultimate place of love. A guaranteed place of rest, peace, and celebration. Heaven is home. It's the promise of being with the One who romanced us into salvation.

I feel so inadequate to describe it. Nor can I. It's all too much for me to comprehend. So let me just put it in the form of a question: How amazing must this God be that we may spend ten thousand years simply adoring Him in awe and wide-eyed wonder? Unconcerned and unaware of time (another earthly concept that will be no more), we are utterly lost for ages in praise.

That's how great heaven is going to be.

In what became his best-known song, former Beatle John Lennon wrote, "Imagine there's no heaven, it's easy if you try." I doubt Lennon would have penned those words had he known how imaginative, exciting, and satisfying heaven will be. Heaven is going to be so great that all of us combined couldn't conceive of its wonder. Scripture doesn't tell us if there will be earthly activities like sports or hobbies. But think of it this way—if those things aren't there, God will provide something much, much better, something that hasn't even been invented yet!

Close your eyes and envision the happiest thought or feeling you've ever had. Got it? Now magnify that thought times a billion and you haven't come close to how great heaven is going to be. And that's based, not on some wishful projection, but on God's gracious revelation to us regarding our future home.

In heaven, we will see Him, know Him, be with Him, serve Him, and reign with Him![58]

No, heaven is not some child's dream. And you definitely can't hallucinate it into existence. It will always be far beyond what you imagine it to be. Thank God, it's way, way better.

Heaven is more than a destination. It's a destiny. More than a place, it's a Person. And what kind of Person would prepare something like this for you? A God who is great. A God who can be trusted. A God who is worthy. A God who loves you way more than you deserve.

God. Loves. You.

His love doesn't cease after salvation and it doesn't diminish when you get to heaven. In fact, your experience of God's love will exponentially increase there.

It's as if He's saying, "All this for you, My bride."

Don't you want to go there?

12

The Beauty Awakes

In Disney's classic *Sleeping Beauty*, young princess Aurora is cursed by an evil sorceress and falls into a deep sleep, out of which she can be awakened only by the kiss of a handsome prince. That's the story most familiar to us. Romantic. Noble. Inspiring. Innocent. However, there's another version closer to the original.

Published in 1634 by Giambattista Basile as *Sun, Moon, and Talia*, this version has a decidedly different tone altogether. After getting a sliver of flax under her fingernail, a young princess, Talia, apparently dies. Her father, a wealthy lord, cannot bear the thought of her death, so he places her on a bed in one of his country mansions. Later, a king out hunting discovers the girl when his falcon flies into the mansion window. Climbing in the window, he discovers the sleeping beauty and, unable to wake the girl, is filled with lust and sexually assaults her. Nine months later, the still asleep princess gives birth to twins, a boy and a girl. Searching for milk, the children end up sucking on her finger, which loosens the flax splinter, waking her up. The king's wife, jealous with rage over what her husband had done, tries to kill the children and have them cooked and served to the king for dinner. However, a compassionate chef saves the children. What follows is more drama as the king has his wife burned alive for attempted murder.[1] He, of course, marries Talia and they live happily ever after.

Um, I think I'll just stick to the Disney version.

In the G-rated cartoon adaptation, the princess was attractive while alive, but seemed even more beautiful in her unconscious state. However, with Jesus's bride it's just the opposite as her spiritual slumber causes her beauty to degenerate. In other words, she is *not* beautiful when she sleeps.

As we previously learned, by the close of the first century, all across Asia Minor Jesus's bride had fallen asleep. And yet, these churches weren't the only ones who were slumbering.[2] So Christ chose to document their lethargy and identify what contributed to their lack of passion and purity for their bridegroom. If we know anything after two thousand years of church history, it's that some things remain constant—namely, Satan's attack on the church and the human nature of those who comprise that church.

Why Christ Rebukes the First-Century Church

So how did Satan's animosity and our natural tendency to wander play itself out in the first century? Jesus called them out, but for what reasons?

1. She grew apathetic toward Him (Revelation 2:4). Jesus says to His bride, "You have left your first love." Over time, she grew less and less enamored with her bridegroom. The honeymoon was over. The newness had worn off. Oh, they still "did church," but Jesus was no longer the main attraction. Other loves and lovers, including self, now occupied her mind, energy, and attention. At first glance, she may not have looked unfaithful, but her heart revealed another story.

What about your church? Or mine? When we gather, is Jesus the focus? Or is the service itself emphasized more? Are we more impressed with the music, the venue, and the teaching or with the Lord Himself? Do we leave each week equipped, challenged, and inspired to fall more passionately in love with our Savior? If not, then either we have fallen out of love with Jesus or our church has. Yes, still betrothed to Him. Still singing about Him. Still using Christian lingo. Still believing the right things about Him. Still planning meetings and running ministries. Still programming activities in His name. Still doing church. But no longer head over heels in love with Him. In other words, asleep.

2. She tolerated false teaching (Revelation 2:14-20). The early church dealt with a variety of false teaching and false teachers. Most of Paul's epistles were written to confront and correct these errors. Today, with the emergence of feel-good preachers and an obsession with being relevant to culture, we've seen a decline in biblical teaching among many churches. This isn't to say we've tossed out the Bible. It's just that Scripture is viewed more as a self-help book and how-to manual for life rather than as a revelation from God.

I fear we've lost a sense of reverence for the Word (and thus the God of the Word). Many pastors cherry-pick passages solely for addressing felt needs. And while we should certainly teach believers how Scripture relates to everyday life, other weighty or less obviously relevant portions of the Bible are neglected. But according to Paul, "*All* Scripture is inspired by God and profitable."[3] Pastors and teachers are still tasked with equipping the saints with "the whole purpose of God."[4]

Read Paul's final passionate plea to young pastor Timothy just before the veteran apostle left this world for heaven:

> I solemnly charge you in the presence of God and of Christ Jesus, who is to judge the living and the dead, and by His appearing and His kingdom: preach the word; be ready in season and out of season; reprove, rebuke, exhort, with great patience and instruction. For the time will come when they will not endure sound doctrine; but wanting to have their ears tickled, they will accumulate for themselves teachers in accordance to their own

desires, and will turn away their ears from the truth and will turn aside to myths. But you, be sober in all things, endure hardship, do the work of an evangelist, fulfill your ministry.[5]

It's clear from Paul that explaining the Word is a high priority not to be taken lightly. He even invokes the judgment seat of Christ as motivation, exhorting Timothy to be faithful in preaching, even when it's "out of season"—even when it's unpopular or considered archaic or passé to do so. In an effort to reach others and make the Bible interesting, we may set aside teaching the Word for a presentation that's a little more stimulating. Movie clips, elaborate stage sets, props, drama, and media-driven manipulation of people's emotions are too often a pastor's "go to," replacing diligent study of the Scripture, spiritual giftedness, and a desperate dependence on the power and illumination of the Spirit.

Of course we can and should be creative. I love creative presentations of Scripture. This isn't a legalism issue but a spiritual integrity issue. Story and creativity are wonderful as long as they anchor and bond the bride to the Scriptures.

God's Word is our only offensive weapon in spiritual battle.[6] We really don't have to make the Bible relevant. It already is because it was written by the creator of language who perfectly understands us and our needs. However, many Christians fail to immerse themselves in their Bible because they don't feel equipped to understand it for themselves. But by being exposed to great teaching and with some personal effort, any believer can understand the Bible.

Today's lack of biblical understanding is one reason why many Christians feel so spiritually powerless, ineffective, and disconnected from God. And this makes them susceptible to false teaching. Paul predicted the time would come when feeling good would trump sound teaching. To combat this theological error, Paul urged

Timothy to be "constantly nourished on the words of the faith and of the sound doctrine which you have been following."[7]

Sound teaching is very important to Jesus because God is very concerned that our thoughts and beliefs accurately represent Him and His truth. But in the absence of solid Bible teaching, we become misguided and confused, and may end up unknowingly worshipping a false image of God. Our understanding of Jesus, truth, and the Christian life can become distorted as we invent our own ideas about God and life based on our feelings or personal thoughts.

One way to remedy this is to place yourself under the ministry of a solid Bible teacher. Doing this, says Paul, builds you up in your faith, allowing you to grow into maturity. It also saves you from being "carried about by every wind of doctrine, by the trickery of men, by craftiness in deceitful scheming."[8] Because we live in a world where many speak and write about the Bible, being equipped in sound teaching is how you learn to discern God's truth from satanic deception and human error.

3. She acted like she was awake and alive, but in reality she was asleep and dead (Revelation 3:1-2). She had movement, just not life! We can also fall into that trap today. Churches can easily slip into busyness that soon makes them more of a business than a body. More ministries. More services. More campuses. More mission trips. More committee meetings. More special events. More concerts. The church is doing stuff all the time, but more is not always better. Sometimes less is more. Lots of activity may give the impression that the church is alive and well, and to be fair, it actually may be. But the life Jesus seeks in His bride is less about deeds and more about devotion.

We see this in microcosm through Jesus's encounter with Mary and Martha.[9] During His visit, Martha kept herself busy serving Christ and others, while Mary was content to mostly sit at Jesus's feet, to be with Him and to soak up truth from Him. But Jesus rebuked Martha for her misplaced priorities and what, in reality, were nothing more than needless distractions.

> But the Lord answered and said to her, "Martha, Martha, you are worried and bothered about so many things; but only one thing is necessary, for Mary has chosen the good part, which shall not be taken away from her."

Martha equated faith with service and activity. But Jesus showed her something better than being busy for Him. Christ desires a bride who can declutter, focusing on what's really important. Though it may require an "act of congress," simplifying the church would greatly reduce the stress level for most pastors and their congregations, while at the same time enhancing their ability to zero in on being with Jesus, hearing from Him, and falling more in love with Him. The main thing is to keep the main thing the main thing!

4. She was lukewarm (Revelation 3:15-16). By the close of the first century, the church was flat, room temperature, no different from the world. We looked into this in-depth in chapter 3. A Christian or church with no visible passion or desperation for Jesus is ineffective in His eyes. He has no use for such lukewarmness. It's salt that has become tasteless.[10] More about this in a bit.

5. She thought she was something when she was nothing (Revelation 3:17). Self-sufficiency is poison, both personally as well as for a church. It's a deceptive spirit, unconsciously birthing the belief that God is no longer an indispensable requirement for church. Christians today rail against society and government for removing God from schools and the public square. But have we been guilty of the same crime? Have we effectively pushed Christ to the margins of His own church? Have we gradually reduced our need for God while incrementally increasing our dependence on ourselves and our own resources?

How radically different this is compared to John the Baptist's life refrain, "He must increase, but I must decrease."[11] That attitude was more than a pithy slogan for John to use when trying to impress his disciples. No, this statement came from the same man who made sure his potential admirers knew he was not the Christ nor Elijah nor the Prophet. "I'm just a voice," he said. "In fact, I am *so not* the Christ that I consider myself unworthy to even untie His shoelace."[12] Then he backed up those words by spending the rest of his life promoting the only One who deserved peoples' attention. And that's one reason Jesus said, "Truly I say to you, among those born of women" (and that pretty much covers everybody) "there has not arisen anyone greater than John the Baptist!"[13] And yet He goes on to add that John, merely a "friend of the bridegroom," is not greater than the least among His humble bride.[14] Our privileges as the bride are greater than John's as the groomsman.

Prestige, power, possessions, and pride are words used by many skeptics and unbelievers to describe the American church today. There's no shortage of celebrity pastors with egos as big and deep as the debt on the buildings they persuaded their congregations to buy into. I've met so many arrogant Christian celebrities over the years that when I meet a genuinely humble Christian leader, I am almost shocked. And this cocky attitude is often leaked to the congregation as a whole. Members begin, consciously or subconsciously, to think their church is the coolest, richest, biggest, hippest, and best. They look down their noses with pity on other congregations that are not like them. That's the pathway to pharisaism.

Years ago, my wife reminded me that how I treat the college intern who picks me up at the airport for a speaking engagement says more about me than anything I later say from a stage. And for humility to be real, it must be embraced. Paul encouraged every believer "not to think more highly of himself than he ought to think; but to think so as to have sound judgment."[15] That doesn't mean we act like we're a worm. And it doesn't mean we deny accomplishments, abilities, successes, or wins. It just means we know at the end of the day we're just a voice pointing to Someone far more important than we are.

I wonder what would happen if Jesus's bride spent less time admiring herself in the mirror and more time being a mirror that reflects Jesus to a world in desperate need of Him.

Surveying the church at the close of the first millennium, we see the bride drifting without anchor in many areas. This leads her into an encounter with an upset Christ who, due to His great love and jealousy for His bride, calls her back to Himself. It's easy to see many of these parallels in the church today. And for that reason alone, Revelation is a deeply relevant book for the last days' church.

Impressing Jesus

Jesus's rebuke of these churches is not, however, without some genuine praise as well. In addition to His condemnation, there is also commendation. He praises some of the churches for their endurance, doctrinal discernment, love, faith, and service. In fact, the churches at Smyrna and Philadelphia received no rebuke from Christ at all. Instead, He praises them for their perseverance under tribulation, obedience, and steadfastness in standing strong for His name. He then exhorts those two churches to be faithful and to overcome.[16]

There's certainly no shortage of church bashing today, and it can be debated which of it is justified or deserved. But we're not talking about a ranting blogger or secular opinion here. Jesus Himself is the One who delivers these scathing reproofs, reminding the church at Laodicea, "Those whom I love, I reprove and discipline."[17]

So His rebuke is not only a good thing, it's actually a way He demonstrates His love for us. It proves we belong to Him. Jesus is jealous for His bride, and He knows all too well how she is prone to wander. Without His Spirit revealing her wayward deeds, the church will continue to stray. Pastors and elder boards cannot keep the church pure by themselves. The body itself must pursue purity as well. From pastor to parishioner, the bride must cry out with a poverty of spirit, confessing her abandonment to the Holy Spirit for divine leadership and enablement.

The church of Scripture is so much more than an organization or a business. She is a living organism and a beautiful bride. My wife's greatest gift to me is not to organize herself or program her day, but to genuinely love me. And according to Paul, Christ loves His church through helping her "sanctify" herself in purity.[18] Every local church (and individual believer) exists primarily to set herself apart and prepare herself for her bridegroom. Vastly more important than what we or our church may ever do for Jesus is who we become for Him.

Service is secondary to submission.[19]

A church's résumé should never eclipse her loyal heart devotion to Christ. We must be known for more than our Sunday services, community work, activities, buildings, cutting-edge technology, music, location, size, budget, or pastor's notoriety.

Rather, the reputation we seek is a fanatical, revolutionary love for our bridegroom.[20] Nothing else really matters.

Above serving the community or even reaching the lost, our highest priority is to be a soul-captivating devotion to Christ. Obedience naturally flows from this kind of love.[21] So we must focus on loving Him. Second to this is an uncommon love for one another. That's how the world knows our Christ is the real deal.[22]

The Jesus of Revelation is not impressed with our "new and improved" brand of Christianity. He's not looking for a big budget; He seeks a beautiful bride. He yawns at our elaborate planning meetings and instead yearns for us to prepare ourselves for His return. This is the bride He is coming to meet in the clouds. All our bridal accessories will be left behind. The only thing He's interested in is the bride herself. At the Rapture, she will shed every vestige of earthly life and ministry to be rescued up to heaven prior to God's wrath being released.

A New Day

So how does the bride (and you and I) prepare herself for that day? Fortunately, we don't have to guess at the answer. Jesus tells us in plain language.

"Wake Up" (Revelation 3:2)

Transitioning from snoozing to real spirituality is a matter of obedience, motivated out of a heart of love.[23] Therefore, Christ issues a stern warning to those churches who fail to come out of hibernation. "Hear My words and rouse out of your slumber," He says, "or else I am coming to you and will remove your lampstand out of its place—unless you repent."[24] And without a lampstand (spiritual influence) what awaits her is a regrettable experience at the bema.[25]

To help us wake up, Jesus invites us to remember.[26] But remember what, Lord? Remember where and what we once were and remember what Jesus has done for us. We're told often in Scripture to remember, primarily because we are prone to forget. "Remember Me and My sacrifice for you," Jesus says.[27] When we consider how He saved us and why, what He saved us from, and what He is preparing for us, how can we remain drowsy?

How?

"Rise Up" (Revelation 3:3,19)

Jesus next urges His bride to repent. But wait, isn't repentance just for sinners? Why would Christians need to repent? The Greek word refers to a "change of mind," which in Scripture results in a change of life. It means we change the way we think about Jesus and our relationship with Him. As we become aware of our sin, John urges us to confess them to God, to agree with Him about our sin. We do this in order to experience the forgiveness He provided at our salvation through Jesus's cross.[28] This same John heard Jesus advise the church at Laodicea to "be zealous and repent."[29]

Repentance and confession do not save us all over again. Rather, they enable us to enjoy our relationship with God. To be zealous means our full heart is in it. We can't recharge or reenter a relationship with Christ unless our whole being is on board. Making halfhearted or empty promises to God only prompts Him to call us fools.[30] Repentance means we've heard Christ, made an honest evaluation of our life, and turned back to Him. It helps us rise up so we can walk with Him. It's normal to regularly turn back to God because we regularly turn away from Him. Therefore, repentance is a natural process in our sanctification, our continual conformity and transformation into the image of Christ.[31]

Jesus also counseled the Ephesian Christians to "do the deeds you did at first."[32] He wanted them to return to the basics—to the simplicity that marks every new believer. Historically, for the Ephesians, that included a strong desire to learn and grow in their faith, practicing repentance, a deep reverence for God's Word, and healthy Christian relationships.[33] We could use more of this in the church today.

"Look Up" (Revelation 2:7,17,28; 3:5,12)

Repenting also helps us overcome ourselves and the world we face each day. And yet, as we witness history gradually transition into earth's final season and the last days, we should be filled, not with dread or anxiety, but with expectancy.[34] Our salvation motivates us to be "looking for the blessed hope and the appearing of the glory of our great God and Savior, Christ Jesus."[35] In looking up, we look forward to the Day when we're rewarded with the presence and promise of Christ. That's why Paul wrote, "knowing the time, that it is already the hour for you to awaken from sleep; for now salvation is nearer to us than when we believed. The night is almost gone, and the day is near. Therefore let us lay aside the deeds of darkness and put on the armor of light."[36]

Concerning the last days, he reminded the Thessalonian disciples, "so then let us not sleep as others do, but let us be alert and sober."[37] Unfortunately, he says, some will sleep, remaining unaware. Unconscious. Out of it. Spiritually clueless. Don't be that Christian.

However, in stark contrast to those slumbering saints, Scripture admonishes us to be:

- sober and alert[38]
- pure in spirit and life[39]
- prepared and unashamed[40]
- comforted and encouraged, full of hope[41]

All these truths are priceless gifts from God, giving us eternal perspective on our short earthly lives. They tell us our days here are numbered. And as we understand the transient nature of our lives, these truths inspire us to redeem the time, spending it wisely, not wasting our lives on trivial pursuits.[42] We have no promise of tomorrow. Our lives are but a vapor, a breath, a wisp of smoke. And we can't allow pride to convince us we have all the time in the world.[43] Christian, this present earth is not our home. We are merely passing through on a journey toward a new heaven and a new, better earth.

This perspective also reminds us Jesus *is* coming back, and perhaps soon. Realizing our time is limited and viewing Jesus's return as imminent causes us to live a life filled with urgency, hope and purpose.

But Revelation's present truths and future prophecies also remind us that God has entrusted us with specific stewardships.[44] It compels us to ask, "What have I been given? What has God loaned to me while I'm here?" Spouse. Children. Family. Time. Abilities. Spiritual giftedness. A circle of influence. Position. Possessions. Money. The gospel. "Am I doing the best with what He has entrusted to me?" In life, there's no yesterday or tomorrow. Only right now. And our future rewards are based on what we do with what we've been given here.[45] Make your life count for Him!

No church or individual Christian is without faults or areas of imperfection. We all struggle. But that doesn't mean all churches (or Christians) are asleep. I'm thankful that many are waking up and returning to the beauty and simplicity of vintage Christianity. This is why Jesus said to the Laodicean church, "Behold, I stand at the door and knock; if anyone hears My voice and opens the door, I will come in to him and will dine with him, and he with Me."[46]

Christ is saying, "Let Me back inside your church and your life. I want to be in charge of My church again. I want your focus to be Me above doing church, reaching the lost, or even loving each other.[47] Do this and we will again enjoy sweet fellowship together."

These churches, the "Revelation Seven," represent all churches not only in John's day but also in ours.[48] Thus Revelation is a book for the bride today. For you and for me. And more than ever as we ramp up to the end times. Then, as now, Christ concludes His messages to the churches with the same admonishment: "He who has an ear, let him hear what the Spirit says to the churches."[49]

He wants to know whether we're really listening to Him. Are we actually taking His words to heart? "Don't miss or dismiss this," Jesus says. "Don't gloss over My message to My church. Please pay close attention to My final written words to last days' believers!"

To show indifference to Jesus's Revelation warning is to remain asleep. Worse, it's willful disobedience or perhaps an indication that there may be no life in the body.

When I die, I want my tank on empty, having wasted nothing. Until then, I'm swinging for the fence. I intend to round third base running full speed, sweat dripping off my brow, crowd on its feet, cheering as I slide into home plate in a cloud of glory dust.

What about you?

Years ago, my wife and I were married in an old cathedral in downtown Little Rock. I have two distinct memories of that epic day. One is the event itself, documented in a photo album residing somewhere in our home. For some reason, this church had a policy that no video or audio could be used during a wedding ceremony. Only photographs. Did I mention we were married in the Stone Age?

The other vivid memory is when, after the preacher and I walked to the altar and the wedding party had made its way down the aisle, the time came for the bride to appear. The rehearsal was over. The bridesmaids stood waiting. There were no more preparations to be made. Everything was ready. The groom had arrived. The bride was prepared.

The day had come.

As the congregation stood in unison to honor the bride, two large wooden doors slowly opened in the back. Beverly and her dad appeared in the huge doorway, whereupon the cathedral's massive pipe organ exploded with Henry Purcell's "Trumpet Voluntary." Because some of the pipes were located right over that doorway, I remember seeing my future father-in-law jump about a foot off the ground. He was awake!

The next thing I remember was Beverly's striking appearance as she gradually made her way down the aisle. She had chosen to wear her mother's wedding gown, perfectly preserved from thirty years earlier. That's when a grapefruit-sized lump formed in my throat. Attempting to choke back the tears, I silently whispered, "O God, she is so beautiful! So pure!"

And then, unexpectedly, my spirit sensed the Lord saying, "Jeff, that's exactly how I see you. Clothed in My righteousness. Pure and prepared for Me and My return."

I had patiently waited nine months for that awesome day, having worked overtime and saved every penny I earned to buy Beverly an engagement ring. Now that anticipated day had arrived and I could not have been any happier. All I wanted was to marry that girl and spend the rest of my life with her.

And all Jesus wants is for His beautiful bride to be awake and ready for Him.

At the conclusion of John's Revelation vision, the apostle is assured that every word he has heard is "faithful and true" and that the prophetic events of Revelation "must soon take place."[50] In other words, Jesus's return is unpredictable and will happen suddenly. Thus the next verse, "And behold, I am coming quickly," followed by the promise, "Blessed is he who heeds the words of the prophecy of this book."

Revelation is meant to be open and read because "the time is near." And just in case we didn't get it, Christ's wake-up call is repeated: "Behold, I am coming quickly, and My reward is with Me."[51]

The Holy Spirit and the bride invite anyone who is listening to these prophecies and who is thirsty for eternal life to "come."[52]

"Yes," Jesus affirms again, "I am coming quickly." To which John responds, "Amen. Come, Lord Jesus."[53]

Our prophetic climb has been arduous at times, but I trust the view and benefits have been worth the effort. Pretty decent view from up here, wouldn't you agree?

Jesus's voice today trumpets reveille to a drowsy bride. It's a clarion call, jolting us to attention and rousing us all out of our collective slumber. This voice is a familiar one. We've heard it thousands of times before. Calling in our spirit. Reviving us. Rescuing from danger. Romancing us back to Him. Confronting us in our sin. Comforting us in our confusion. Challenging us toward the next faith adventure. Whispering to us in the pain of our darkest hours, "I'm still here. Right here beside you. I'm never leaving you."

It's that same voice calling to us right now, awakening us to a new day in our life with Him.

Wake up. Rise up. Look up!

And it's a voice we will hear again, maybe soon. A voice calling us skyward.

Beloved, behold, your bridegroom comes.

Wake up, bride!

Make yourself ready!

Notes

Introduction

1. Revelation 1:1.
2. Romans 11:33-36.
3. John 14:1-3.
4. Revelation 22:20.

Chapter 1: A Day Is Coming

1. For example, Isaiah's prophecy (chapter 53) concerning the redemptive work of the future suffering Messiah occurred during a time of spiritual anemia and apostasy.

2. Ezekiel 33:1-7.

3. Mark 13 (ESV).

4. Mark 14:37-42 (emphasis added).

5. Matthew 25:1-13.

6. While I believe this parable specifically points toward those alive during the Tribulation at the time of Jesus's Second Coming, the principle remains true for those of us alive today. Be ready.

7. Acts 20:7-12.

8. Ephesians 6:18.

9. 1 Thessalonians 5:6.

10. 1 Peter 1:13.

11. 1 Peter 4:7.

12. There are divergent views regarding the end times and the interpretations of Revelation and end-times prophecy. There are many I greatly respect but disagree with regarding what Scripture says about the Tribulation, Christ's return, and His future kingdom. I encourage you to carefully examine all major interpretations and decide for yourself.

13. Revelation 1:3; 2 Timothy 3:16.

14. Revelation 22:20; 1 Corinthians 16:22 (*Maranatha* means "Our Lord, come!").

15. Titus 2:13.

16. For a more detailed description of this incident, see "On Walkabout at the Franklin Mountains B-36 Crash Site," *On Walkabout* (blog), January 25, 2010, http://on-walkabout.com/2010/01/25/exploring-the-franklin-mountains-b-36-crash-site/.

Chapter 2: The "New" Jesus

1. Jude 14,17-18.

2. Prophecy does many things for us:

   • Helps us understand the times we live in (1 Chronicles 12:32).

   • Calms our fears about the future (Matthew 28:20; John 14:1-3,27).

   • Gives us confidence, courage, and comfort in the present (1 Thessalonians 4:13-18; John 16:33).

   • Increases our faith in God who's in control of earth's story (Isaiah 40:12-26; Psalm 115:3; Daniel 4:35).

   • Helps us see the relevance of our Bible to life, both for now and the future (2 Timothy 3:16-17; 2 Peter 1:20-21).

   • Builds expectancy and anticipation for what is to come (Revelation 22:10; Matthew 6:10).

   • Gives us positive hope in a hopeless world, rescuing us from despair (Titus 2:13-15).

   • Keeps us centered in an age of doctrinal error, heresy, and apostasy (1 Timothy 4:1; 2 Timothy 3:1-17).

   • Blesses us as we listen and obey Scripture's prophetic words (Revelation 1:3).

   • Motivates us to be urgent about our mission here on earth, not wasting our time on worthless pursuits (Ephesians 5:15-16).

   • Fuels the fire of our desire to see others know Jesus (2 Corinthians 5:10-13; 6:2).

   • Gives us perspective on the temporary nature of suffering (John 16:1,4; Romans 8:18).

   • Helps us prioritize spiritual things over physical things, living wisely (Psalm 90:10-12).

   • Purifies our lives as we prepare ourselves as Christ's bride (1 John 3:2-3).

   • Helps us know what to expect as we live for God in an increasingly hostile world (John 15:18-23).

3. Revelation 22:12.

4. Matthew 2:16.

5. Revelation 1:1-20.

6. Most likely exiled there by the Roman emperor Domitian, who reigned from AD 81–96.

7. Revelation 1:1.

8. Revelation 1:8; 22:13.

9. John 1:1,14,18; 8:58; 14:6; Colossians 1:15-19; 2:9; Hebrews 1:3,8.

10. Revelation 1:1.

11. Revelation 1:7; Daniel 7:13; Zechariah 12:10.

12. This could also be accomplished in some supernatural manner as well.

13. Matthew 5:18, where Jesus applies this to the Old Testament. Revelation 1:5; 1:18-19; 4:1; 21:5.

14. Romans 11:26.

15. Colossians 1:16.

16. Colossians 1:17.

17. Revelation 1:13.

18. Hebrews 4:14; Daniel 7:9; Matthew 25:31-46; 2 Timothy 4:1.

19. Revelation 1:14.

20. Proverbs 16:31.

21. Colossians 2:13.

22. 1 Corinthians 3:13.

23. Hebrews 4:13.

24. Revelation 19:12.

25. Revelation 1:15.

26. Exodus 38:1-7.
27. 2 Peter 3:4-9.
28. Revelation 1:10.
29. Revelation 1:15.
30. Ezekiel 43:2.
31. Revelation 1:16.
32. Revelation 2:12,16; 19:15.
33. Revelation 1:16 (NIV).
34. Touch—Song of Songs 5:4-5; 7:6-9; Proverbs 5:19; sound—Psalm 89:15; Isaiah 52:7; 1 Thessalonians 4:16; Revelation 4, 21; sight—Proverbs 7:10-17; Luke 7:21; smell—Ephesians 5:2; Philippians 4:18; Song of Songs 1:12; Exodus 30; Psalm 141:2; Revelation 5:8; taste—Psalm 19:10; 34:8.
35. Ecclesiastes 2:25.
36. Revelation 1:17; Genesis 17:3; Numbers 16:22; Daniel 8:17-18,27; Acts 9:4.
37. Revelation 1:17.
38. 1 Corinthians 15:50-58.
39. Revelation 1:18.
40. John 20:19ff; 21:1-3.
41. 1 Corinthians 15:17-19.
42. John 4:13.

43. 1 Corinthians 15:1-7.
44. www.ccel.org/ccel/schaff/anf03.txt. Tertullian lived from AD 160–230.
45. Apostles and early Christians were ostracized, tortured, and killed for their faith. This was certainly evidence of their unwavering faith in their resurrected Lord. Aside from merely being sincere, many of the first-century Christians were eyewitnesses to the truth of the resurrection. This fact, combined with many other proofs (including the inability of two thousand years of skeptics' theories attempting to explain away this event) provide a solid intellectual and historical foundation for this faith in Jesus.
46. Revelation 19:16.
47. Job 14:15.
48. Job 14:5; Psalm 139:16.
49. Deuteronomy 29:29; Romans 11:33-36.
50. James 4:6.
51. Revelation 1:19.
52. Revelation 1:3.
53. Revelation 1:3.

Chapter 3: Wedding Dress

1. The Greek word for "church" literally means this.
2. Of Paul's thirteen letters, nine are to churches, and at least three others are to church leaders.
3. 1 Corinthians 12:12-27.
4. Approximately 85% of churches in America have less than two hundred people. 60% of those are under one hundred people. The average congregation size in the US is just eighty-nine people. Smyrna may have been about that size.
5. Revelation 3:15-16.
6. Luke 14:34-35 (NIV).
7. Revelation 3:17.
8. Revelation 3:18.
9. 2 Timothy 2:13.
10. Revelation 3:19; Hebrews 12:5-11.

11. Revelation 2:15. The "lampstand" is a church's ability to shine Christ's light and influence others for the kingdom.

12. Revelation 3:18-19.

13. The Greek word *metanoia* comes from two Greek words: *meta* ("after") and *noia* ("mind"). When combined, the word means to think something in your *mind* that produces a change *after* you think it. Hence, in a biblical context, a "change of mind leading to a change of lifestyle."

14. Revelation 3:20.

15. John 13:12,23.

16. Revelation 3:21.

17. Romans 8:37-39; 1 John 5:5.

18. Revelation 1:6; Matthew 19:28; Luke 22:29-30.

19. 2 Corinthians 11:2-3.

Chapter 4: Grounding the Rapture

1. 1 Thessalonians 4:13-18.

2. *Rapiemur* and *rapturo* are two forms of the same verb, *rapio*—"to catch or seize" (among other definitions).

3. Revelation 6:16-17. Though believers in the Tribulation are not the target of God's wrath, they will be affected by the fallout and aftershocks of His judgments during this time.

4. Romans 8:1; 1 Thessalonians 1:10; 5:9.

5. Psalm 115:3; Job 42:2; Daniel 4:35.

6. This belief was "reborn" due to the Reformation, as it certainly wasn't prevalent at the time.

7. This is documented in a sermon from the fourth century attributed to "Pseudo-Ephraem." The sermon is titled, "On the Last Times, the Antichrist, and the End of the World, or Sermon on the End of the World" (www.pre-trib.org/article-view.php ?id=169). For further study on belief in a pretrib Rapture, see Mark Hitchcock, *The End* (Wheaton, IL: Tyndale House, 2012).

8. *The Didache* is also called *The Teaching of the Twelve Apostles*. Chapter 16:1 states, "Watch concerning your life; let not your lamps be quenched or your loins be loosed, but be ye ready, for ye know not the hour at which our Lord cometh."

9. John Walvoord, *The Rapture Question* (Grand Rapids, MI: Zondervan, 1979).

10. Of the church fathers who condemned Marcion were Justin, Irenaeus, Clement of Alexandria, Origen, and Tertullian.

11. Justin Martyr, "First Apology," *Ante-Nicene Fathers*, vol. 1, 183.

12. Isaiah 7:14; Matthew 2:17-18; Luke 2:12; Acts 1:6-8,12; 2:1-13.

13. Ezekiel 37–38.

14. Though many respected scholars, theologians, authors, and prominent pastors hold to a strong belief in the Rapture, this is not our ultimate authority. Other godly men and even whole denominations see Revelation as purely symbolic and the Rapture as nonexistent. However, I believe there is strong biblical and theological evidence to support belief in the Rapture.

Chapter 5: The Bridegroom Comes!

1. Revelation 6:16-17.

2. One view of the Tribulation states that the events of Revelation 6–19 were fulfilled in the first century. Known as the preterist view, it considers much of Revelation to be symbolic while other passages are seen as having been literally fulfilled. Nero would be the Antichrist and the Tribulation would have ended in AD 70 with the destruction of the Jewish temple. Jesus's return was in the clouds after witnessing this destruction. Other traditions see almost all of Revelation as purely symbolic. Chief among these are amillennialists, who don't believe in an actual, literal reign of Jesus on the earth following His return.

3. Interpreting the Bible "literally" means understanding it in light of its linguistic, grammatical, historical, cultural, and contextual setting. Symbols and figures of speech (similes, metaphors) are interpreted plainly. We understand and interpret each passage for what it is saying, at face value, unless there are sufficient grammatical or contextual reasons to see it as symbolic.

4. Other passages that reference the Rapture are: John 14:1-3; Romans 8:19; 1 Corinthians 1:7-8; 15:51-53; 16:22; Philippians 3:20-21; 4:5; Colossians 3:4; 1 Thessalonians 1:10; 2:19; 4:13-18; 5:9,23; 2 Thessalonians 2:1,3; 1 Timothy 6:4; 2 Timothy 4:1,8; Titus 2:13; Hebrews 9:28; James 5:7-9; 1 Peter 1:7,13; 5:4; 1 John 2:28-3:2; Jude 21; Revelation 3:10.

5. Revelation 3:10.

6. 1 Timothy 4:1; 2 Timothy 3:1; James 5:3; 1 Peter 1:20; 2 Peter 3:3; Hebrews 1:2; 1 John 2:18.

7. Matthew 16:1-4.

8. John 14:1-3 (NIV).

9. John 2:1-11. I wonder if Jesus thought of His future bride while at this wedding.

10. John 6:44; 17:2,6,9,24.

11. 1 Corinthians 6:20; 7:23; Revelation 5:9; Acts 20:28.

12. Matthew 1:19-20; 5:31.

13. A trumpet-like instrument, usually made from a ram's horn.

14. John 14:1-3 (NIV).

15. Ephesians 5:22-33; 2 Corinthians 11:1-3.

16. Titus 2:13.

17. 1 John 3:2.

18. 1 Thessalonians 4:13; 2 Thessalonians 2:1-5.

19. 1 Thessalonians 1:10.

20. 1 Thessalonians 5:9.

21. 1 Thessalonians 4:13-17.

22. John 11:43.

23. Daniel 10:13; Jude 9.

24. Daniel 10:13.

25. Daniel 10:21; 12:1; Revelation 12:7.

26. Matthew 25:6.

27. Exodus 19:16-19; Numbers 10:1-3.

28. 1 Corinthians 15:51-52.

29. 1 Corinthians 15:51-55.

30. 1 Corinthians 15:35-54.

31. Following His resurrection, Jesus was recognizable, walked, ate, and did other common human things (Luke 24:39; 24:42-43; John 20:25-29). But He also could apparently appear and reappear at will (John 20:19,26).

32. *Theological Dictionary of the New Testament* (Grand Rapids, MI: William B. Eerdmans Publishing Co., 1985).

33. Acts 8:39-40.

34. 2 Corinthians 12:2,4.

35. Revelation 12:5.

36. Here are all the verses where *harpazo* is used in the NT, along with the meaning in each context: Matthew 11:12—take by force; Matthew 12:29—carry off; Matthew 13:19—snatches away; John 6:15—take by force; John 10:12—snatch by force; John 10:29—snatch by force; Acts 8:39—snatch away, disappear; Acts 23:10—take away by force; 2 Corinthians 12:2—caught up to heaven; 2 Corinthians 12:4—caught up into Paradise; 1 Thessalonians 4:17—caught up…in the clouds; Jude 23—(quickly) snatching out of the fire; Revelation 12:5—(referring to Jesus) caught up to God (at the ascension).

37. Matthew 24:3,27,37,39; 1 Thessalonians 2:19; 3:13; 4:15; 5:23; 2 Thessalonians 2:1,8; 1 Corinthians 15:23; James 5:7-8; 2 Peter 1:16; 3:4,12; 1 John 2:28). It can be argued that all these references refer to the Rapture except for Matthew 24:3,27,37,39; 1 Thessalonians 3:13; 2 Thessalonians 2:8; and 2 Peter 1:16, which refer to Jesus's Second Coming at Armageddon. Therefore, the *parousia* (presence, arrival, coming) of the Lord occurs in two phases. The Rapture, where Jesus comes *for* His bride (1 Thessalonians 4) and the Second Coming, where Jesus comes *with* His bride (1 Thessalonians 3:13; Revelation 19). One is imminent while the other is preceded by seven years of tribulation.

38. 1 Corinthians 15:52 (NIV). It's estimated the average eye blink is about 300-400 milliseconds (or about 0.3 of a second) in duration. However, a *twinkle* is even less than that, only requiring about 100 milliseconds (or 0.1 of a second). But again, Paul gets even more precise here. The word translated "moment" is the Greek *atomo*. This word is used only once in the Bible, and only in reference to the Rapture. *Atomo* refers to "that which cannot be divided" or "an indivisible amount of time."

39. The word *time* here is *kairos*, meaning "era, age."

40. 1 Corinthians 15:51; Revelation 5:9; 7:9.

41. Ephesians 1:4.

42. See Mark 3:14; John 14:3; 17:24; Philippians 1:23; Revelation 17:14.

43. Philippians 2:10-11.

44. 1 John 3:2-3.

45. 1 Thessalonians 4:13.

46. Matthew 7:24-29; Ephesians 4:11-16.

Chapter 6: Gold, Silver, and Bronze

1. 2 Corinthians 5:10.
2. 1 Corinthians 3:13; 4:5.
3. See Matthew 23 for Jesus's scathing rebuke of the religious leaders of His day.
4. John 3:16-18.
5. The word was also used to refer to a legal judgment seat, as in Acts 18:12.
6. 1 Corinthians 4:5.
7. John 5:22.
8. Ephesians 2:8-9.
9. 1 Corinthians 3:13,15; Colossians 2:13-14; Hebrews 10:14.
10. Romans 5:1; 8:1; 2 Corinthians 5:21; Ephesians 1:13; 4:30.
11. 1 Corinthians 3:12-15.
12. 1 Corinthians 4:5.
13. 1 Corinthians 4:4.
14. 1 Samuel 16:7; Hebrews 4:13.
15. 1 Corinthians 9:24.
16. Revelation 4:4.
17. Matthew 10:41.
18. Matthew 25:37-40.
19. Matthew 10:42; Mark 9:41.
20. Luke 19:13-26.
21. Hebrews 12:3-11.
22. Philippians 1:6.
23. The Tribulation saints aren't yet redeemed or in heaven, and Old Testament saints will be resurrected for reward at the Second Coming (Daniel 12:1-3).
24. 2 Corinthians 5:21; Revelation 3:4,18; 4:4; 19:7-8,14.
25. 1 Corinthians 13:12.
26. 1 Timothy 6:17-19; James 1:17.
27. Revelation 5:11-14.
28. Philippians 2:9-11.
29. 2 Corinthians 5:11.
30. 2 Timothy 1:7 (ESV).
31. 1 John 4:18.
32. 2 Corinthians 7:1.
33. Acts 9:31.
34. Proverbs 9:10.
35. 1 Corinthians 3:10-15.
36. 1 Corinthians 2:2.
37. Jeremiah 17:9; 1 Corinthians 4:3-5.
38. In Matthew 5:48, Jesus does say we "are to be perfect, as your heavenly Father is perfect." However, the greater context and theme of the Sermon on the Mount is Christ's teaching of a more complete understanding of Old Testament Law. We know from the New Testament that our perfection is made possible by Jesus's imputation of His righteousness to our account (2 Corinthians 5:21). Practically speaking, our experiential perfection (Greek *teleioi*, "maturity, completion") is guaranteed through our sanctification and ultimate glorification at death or the revelation of Jesus at the Rapture (Philippians 1:6; Romans 8:29-30).
39. Romans 8:18.
40. 1 Corinthians 15:58.

Chapter 7: Meanwhile, in Heaven…a Throne

1. Christians weren't the only people to suffer persecution. Jews also felt the Caesars' iron fist, as did anyone who dared to refuse submission to Roman rule.

2. In two thousand years, nothing has come close to paralleling or fulfilling these prophecies.

3. *Foxes Book of Martyrs: An Edition for the People* (Eaton and Mains, 1911).

4. *The History of Christian Martyrdom, Being an Authentic Account of the Lives, Sufferings, and Deaths of the Protestant Martyrs* (J.S. Virtue & Co., 1881).

5. *Documents of the Christian Church*, ed. Henry Bettenson and Chris Maunder, 3rd. ed. (New York: Oxford University Press, 1999), 2.

6. From Justin Martyr's *Dialogue with Trypho*, Ante-Nicene Christian Library, *Translations of the Writings of the Fathers*, vol. 2 (Edinburgh: T. and T. Clark, 1868), 237.

7. Robert L. Wilkin, "The Piety of the Persecutors," *Christian History* 11, no. 27 (1990): 18.

8. To the unbelieving mind, the spiritual things of God are foolishness, and they cannot understand them. See 1 Corinthians 1:18-25; 2:6-16.

9. Matthew 7:13-14; John 14:6; Acts 9:2.

10. Daniel 2:40-44; 7:7; Revelation 13:1; 17:12.

11. Michael Snyder, "Christians Are Being Burned Alive, Beheaded, Crucified, Tortured to Death and Imprisoned," *Infowars.com*, December 10, 2013, www.infowars.com/christians-are-being-burned-alive-beheaded-cru

cified-tortured-to-death-and-imprisoned-in-metal-shipping-containers/.

12. www.fas.org/irp/eprint/rightwing.pdf.

13. John 15:18-21.

14. Romans 12:2.

15. John 15:22.

16. 1 Peter 3:15-16.

17. Revelation 4:1.

18. Revelation 21:11.

19. Ezekiel 1:28.

20. Regarding white garments, compare Revelation 3:4-5,18; 19:7-8; on crowns, see chapter 6 on our joint-rule with Christ, see Revelation 2:26-27; 3:21; 5:10; Matthew 19:28; Luke 22:30; 1 Corinthians 6:2-3; 2 Timothy 2:12; and ultimately Revelation 20:4,6.

21. Daniel 12:1-3.

22. Matthew 19:27-28; 25:31.

23. Revelation 4:5; 6:1; 8:5; 11:19; 14:2; 16:18; 19:6.

24. We see *seven* repeatedly in Revelation. There are seven spirits (1:4), seven lampstands (1:12), seven stars (1:16), seven churches (chapters 2–3), seven seals (5:1), seven horns (5:6), seven trumpets (8:2), seven heads of the dragon (12:3), seven heads of the beast (13:1), among others.

25. See Revelation 1:4; Genesis 2:2; Exodus 20:10; Leviticus 14:7; Acts 6:3.

26. Isaiah 6:2-3; Ezekiel 1:5-25; 10:1-22.

27. Genesis 3:24.

28. Exodus 25:18-22.

29. Ezekiel 28:14-16.

30. Ezekiel 1:10.

31. Isaiah 6:2 describes seraphim as having six wings, while Ezekiel's angels had only four wings.

32. Hebrews 4:16.

33. Isaiah 6:3.

34. The Hebrew word *qadosh* (translated "holy") primarily means to "be separate," as does its Greek counterpart, *hagios* ("set apart, holy").

35. Isaiah 40:25.

36. Isaiah 55:8-9.

37. This is one of fourteen "praise ceremonies" or "doxologies" recorded in the book of Revelation.

38. Compare Revelation 1:4.

39. Exodus 3:14.

40. Romans 11:36.

41. Revelation 4:11.

42. Genesis 1:1.

43. Colossians 1:15-17.

44. Philippians 2:9-11; Proverbs 16:4; Romans 9:18-23.

45. Ephesians 1:13-14, 4:30.

46. Psalm 46:1-2.

47. Romans 8:18.

Chapter 8: Rebels and Wrath

1. Revelation 5:1.

2. Revelation 5:5.

3. Revelation 5:9-10.

4. John 3:16; Romans 5:18-19; 2 Peter 3:9.

5. Revelation 5:11.

6. Revelation 5:14.

7. 1 Thessalonians 5:1-3.

8. Compare Matthew 24:6-7.

9. Genesis 6:5-6,11-13; see also Matthew 24:37.

10. Compare Matthew 24:7.

11. There are several views concerning these wild beasts. One view states that animals will become ferocious and deadly during the Tribulation due to a thinning food supply brought on by war. The other view sees them as representing the Antichrist and his kingdom leaders who destroy human life. The Greek word itself is explicitly used this latter way elsewhere in Revelation.

12. Matthew 24:7-8; Luke 21:11.

13. Revelation 12:11.

14. Matthew 24:9-10.

15. Matthew 24:7.

16. See Zechariah 14:6-7 and Acts 2:19-20.

17. See Romans 1:18-21; 2:14-16.

18. Isaiah 26:4.

19. Luke 21:11.

20. This "seal" is real, though it's not likely to be a physical mark. Rather, it refers to the spiritual seal God places on authentic believers (2 Corinthians 1:22; Ephesians 1:13; 4:30).

21. Revelation 7:4-8.

22. This is evidenced by the fact that they are portrayed as standing with the Lamb (Jesus) on Mount Zion (Revelation 14:1) and also because of the nature of God's protective seal.

23. Compare Revelation 5:9.

24. Matthew 24:14.

25. Revelation 16:2; 19:20.

26. See Romans 11, specifically vv. 25-27.

27. Revelation 7:9.

28. Revelation 20:4.

29. Verses regarding salvation during the Tribulation include Revelation 6:9; 7:9,14; 20:4 and Matthew 24:14.

30. Revelation 8:5.

31. The Seal, Trumpet, and Bowl Judgments increase in succession and intensity. They also appear to occur more frequently, like birth pangs (Matthew 24:8). Even more convincing is Jesus's statement that the last half of this "tribulation" period (Matthew 24:9) will be the worst in all of human history, even designating it as the "great tribulation" (Matthew 24:21).

32. Compare Exodus 9:23-25.

33. Wormwood is a bitter plant found in the desert. It's mentioned in the Old Testament where it refers to the bitterness of sorrow and judgment (Deuteronomy 29:18; Proverbs 5:4).

34. In Revelation 16:8-9, the sun is heated up again to scorch mankind.

35. Cf. Revelation 4:7.

36. This is the prison where some demons are kept by God (Luke 8:31; 11:7; 17:8; 20:1,3). Satan is later cast into this abyss (Revelation 20:1-3).

37. Genesis 6:1-2; Jude 6-7.

38. Those tormented by demons in the New Testament lose control of themselves, suffering under the demons' rule over them (Mark 9:22). The similarity here is that even the ability to choose death is denied those who bear the mark of the Antichrist.

39. The Bible never records that righteous angels are ever bound, as these four are.

40. Revelation 9:15.

41. Combine Revelation 6:8 with 9:15.

42. Revelation 9:16.

43. See Genesis 19:24,28 where fire and brimstone are used in judgment.

44. Revelation 9:20-21.

45. Jeremiah 17:9; 2 Thessalonians 2:10-12.

46. Deuteronomy 32:17; Psalm 106:36-37; 1 Corinthians 10:20-21.

47. Exodus 20:3-5.

48. John 3:19-21.

49. Robert Thomas, *Revelation 8–22, An Exegetical Commentary* (Chicago: Moody Publishers, 1995), 54.

50. See also Galatians 5:20; Revelation 18:23; 21:8; 22:15.

51. Genesis 6:1-2; 19:1ff. For more on how Noah's world parallels our own, see Jeff Kinley, *As It Was in the Days of Noah* (Eugene, OR: Harvest House Publishers, 2014).

52. Margo Kaplan, "Pedophilia: A Disorder, Not a Crime," *New York Times*, October 5, 2014, www.nytimes.com/2014/10/06/opinion/pedophilia-a-disorder-not-a-crime.html?_r=0. See also John Rossomando, "Conference Aims to Normalize Pedophilia," *Daily Caller,* August 15, 2011, http://dailycaller.com/2011/08/15/conference-aims-to-normalize-pedophilia/.

53. Compare Romans 1:18-32.

54. Revelation 16:10-11.

55. Hebrews 10:26-27.

56. In Scripture, a mystery is simply a truth that hasn't yet been revealed (Ephesians 3:1-10).

57. John is writing/recording Revelation's message as he hears it, rather than from memory (10:4).

58. See Psalm 19:9-10; Jeremiah 15:16-18; Ezekiel 2:9-10; 3:1-4,14.

59. Revelation 10:8-11.

60. Revelation 19–20.

61. Revelation 16:1.

62. The Septuagint (translation of the Old Testament from Hebrew to Greek) uses the same word found here in Revelation to describe the sores that plagued the Egyptians.

63. Remember the Second Trumpet Judgment was similar, yet only contaminated one third of the sea and killing the same percentage of life in it.

64. Exodus 7:20-25.

65. "If All the Ice Melted" (map), *National Geographic*, http://ngm.nationalgeo graphic.com/2013/09/rising-seas/if-ice-melted-map

66. Exodus 10:21-23.

67. Dozens of interpretations have been offered identifying this army from the east, but the most likely explanation is the Chinese military.

68. Exodus 14:21-22.

69. Antichrist will lead a campaign into Egypt (Daniel 11:40-45) as well as lay siege to Jerusalem (Zechariah 14:2) before the final battle at Armageddon (Revelation 16:16).

70. Revelation 16:15. See Matthew 24:43; Luke 12:39 where Jesus compared His Second Coming to the unexpected arrival of a thief. Also 1 Thessalonians 5:2,4 and 2 Peter 3:10.

71. Revelation 16:16.

Chapter 9: Satan's Celebrity

1. The words "caught up" come from the same word used to describe the Rapture of the church in 1 Thessalonians 4:17, here referring to Christ's ascension in Acts 1:9.

2. See Genesis 37:9-11; Isaiah 9:6; Matthew 2:13-15.

3. Revelation 12:3.

4. This is exactly half the days that make up the Tribulation, indicating that this event takes place at the midway point of the seven years. See also Matthew 24:16-20.

5. See Zechariah 13:8-9; Romans 11:25-27.

6. Isaiah 14:12-14 and Ezekiel 28:11-19 give us an inside glimpse into how Lucifer originally became Satan.

7. Jude 9; Deuteronomy 34:5-6.

8. Revelation 12:12.

9. Job 1.

10. Revelation 12:8.

11. Revelation 12:10-12.

12. Revelation 13:1.

13. The Greek word used here signifies a "wild beast" (*therion*) and Antichrist lives up to his name as he goes on a ravenous slaughter, devouring God's people (Daniel 7:21). The false prophet is also called "another beast" (Revelation 13:11).

14. 1 John 2:18.

15. 1 John 2:18-22; 4:3; 2 John 7.

16. John 8:44.

17. Compare Revelation 19:15 with 13:10; 5:6 with 13:1; 5:6 with 13:3,8; 14:1 with 13:16-17; and 1:18 with 13:3.

18. Revelation 13:1.

19. Daniel 2:42-44; 7:7-8,24.

20. Revelation 17:13-14.

21. Daniel 2:42-44; 7:7,24.

22. Revelation 13:1; 17:3,12-14.

23. Daniel 7:24.

24. Daniel 7:8.

25. Compare Daniel 7:8,23-24 and Revelation 17:12.

26. Revelation 17:12-13,17.

27. "The Treaties of Rome (1957)," *Histo riasiglo20.org*, www.historiasiglo20 .org/europe/traroma.htm.

28. Initially called the European Economic Community, later changing its name to the European Union. www .civitas.org.uk/eufacts/FSTREAT/ TR1.php.

29. Daniel 2:35,44; Revelation 17:14; 19:19-21; 20:1-3.

30. Robert Thomas, *Revelation 8-22, An Exegetical Commentary* (Chicago: Moody Press, 1995), 154.

31. Matthew 4:9; Luke 4:6; 2 Corinthians 4:4.

32. Daniel's vision in 2:41-43 illustrates that this final kingdom will have inherent internal problems, mixing strong nations with weaker ones.

33. Revelation 13:1.

34. Revelation 17:13-14.

35. 1 Timothy 6:15; Revelation 19:16.

36. See Revelation 17:15.

37. Revelation 9:1-6,11; 11:7; 17:8.

38. Daniel 11:38.

39. 2 Thessalonians 2:6-9.

40. 1 Thessalonians 5:1-3.

41. Revelation 13:16-17.

42. www.templeinstitute.org/main.htm.

43. The same word for "slain" in 13:3 indicates a violent death, and is used to describe the death of Christ in Revelation 5:6.

44. See also Revelation 13:8,12; 14:9,11; 20:4.

45. Isaiah 14:12-14 and Ezekiel 28:11-19.

46. Revelation 13:4.

47. Exodus 15:11; Psalm 35:10; 113:5; Isaiah 40:18,25; 46:5; Jeremiah 49:19; Micah 7:18.

48. 2 Thessalonians 2:4 (NLT).

49. Revelation 13:12-15.

50. Revelation 12:13-17.

51. Revelation 13:3-4,15.

52. Revelation 13:7-10,15. Not all these will die, as some will enter the millennial kingdom alive (Matthew 25:31-46; Isaiah 65:20-25).

53. Revelation 13:8.

54. Ephesians 1:4-5; Philippians 4:3; 1 Peter 1:19-20; Revelation 3:5; 17:8; 20:12,15; 21:27.

55. Revelation 13:9 adds the admonition, "if anyone has an ear, let him hear," but does not include the phrase "what the Spirit says to the churches," as seen combined elsewhere in John's Revelation when speaking to the church (2:7; 3:6,13,22). Compare this with Jesus's promise to the church in Philadelphia to "keep you from the hour of testing, that hour which is about to come upon the whole world" (3:10).

56. Revelation 13:10.

57. The aorist tense of this Greek verb translated "blaspheme" indicates an ongoing action, meaning his blasphemy extends the length of his career. (See Thomas, *Revelation 8-22*, 161).

58. 1 Peter 5:8-9.

59. Revelation 16:13; 19:20; 20:10.

60. Matthew 24:24.

61. John 16:13-15.

62. Revelation 13:13-14; see also Genesis 3:1-7; Revelation 12:9.

63. 1 John 4:1-3.

64. 2 Corinthians 11:14.

65. Revelation 13:16-17.

66. Matthew 24:21.

67. James Moulton, George Milligan, *The Vocabulary of The Greek Testament* (Grand Rapids, MI: Wm. B. Eerdmans Publishing, 1982), 683.

68. Revelation 13:18.

69. The number *six* is associated with man in Scripture (created on the sixth day), while *seven* is the number

of perfection (God rested on the seventh day, seventh day was the Sabbath, seven repeatedly used throughout Revelation).

70. See "Stick-On Tattoos Go Electric," *National Science Foundation*, August 11, 2011, www.nsf.gov/news/news_summ .jsp?cntn_id=121343; "The FDA Approved RFID Tags for Human Use," *NODISINFO.COM*, October 8, 2013, http://nodisinfo.com/fda-approved-rfid-tags-human-use/; "Invisible RFID Ink Safe for Cattle and People, Company Says," *InformationWeek*, January 10, 2007, www.informationweek .com/invisible-rfid-ink-safe-for-cattle -and-people-company-says/d/d-id/105 0602?.

71. It is also possible that Antichrist's mark won't involve biomedical or modern technology, but simply be a hard to replicate stamp or tattoo of some type, perhaps modeled after the tattoos used to mark slaves in biblical times.

72. 2 Thessalonians 2:10-12.

73. Revelation 14:9-11.

74. Isaiah 40:21-25.

75. Matthew 10:28.

76. Revelation 4.

77. Mark Hitchcock, *The End* (Wheaton, IL: Tyndale, 2012), 258.

78. Antichrist's reign of terror is limited by God to forty-two months (Revelation 13:5). God, as always, is sovereign over governments (Daniel 4:17,25,32).

Chapter 10: Return Engagement!

1. Revelation 17:1,5.

2. "Babylon" is mentioned nearly three hundred times in the Bible.

3. In Genesis 11, earth's inhabitants were led by a mighty warrior named Nimrod. He eventually established a kingdom, beginning in Shinar.

4. Genesis 11:4.

5. Later, the Babylonians would refer to Babel as the "gate of God."

6. The book of Daniel takes place during Nebuchadnezzar's reign in the kingdom of Babylon. According to Revelation 9:14, four demonic entities are currently being held at the Euphrates River (the location of Babylon) waiting to be released in the Sixth Trumpet Judgment. Also compare Zechariah 5:5-11 with Revelation 17–18.

7. In Revelation 16:19 and 17:18, John takes time to point out when a geographical location is meant to be understood in symbolic terms (see Revelation 11:8). All other locations are literal (Isle of Patmos, seven churches in chapters 2–3, Armageddon).

8. Matthew 7:13-14, 21-23.

9. This religious emphasis will no doubt be very ecumenical, and in light of Christ's exclusivist claims to deity, potentially embrace a blend of many religions, including the damning doctrine of universalism (the belief that everyone goes to heaven).

10. Genesis 3:1-7.

11. Revelation 17:6,16. We know from Revelation 13 that Antichrist will eventually require the world to worship him at Tribulation's midpoint, so the false religious system of Babylon must exist during the *first* three and a half years.

12. Revelation 17:1,15.

13. See Revelation 18. A city rising out of the Plain of Shinar is not at all a far-fetched proposition considering the context of the difficult times that will follow the Rapture, the sudden rise to power of Antichrist, and some of the world's richest oil reserves located in that region.

14. Revelation 18:2,5.

15. Revelation 16:19; 18:16-24.

16. Revelation 17:4,6; 18:3,6.

17. Revelation 16:16.

18. Though the word itself is used only once, the War (Campaign) of Armageddon is predicted many times in Scripture (Isaiah 34:1-16; 63:1-6; Joel 3:1-17; Zechariah 12:1-9; 14:1-15; Malachi 4:1-5; Revelation 14:14-20; 16:12-16; 19:19-21). This area of Megiddo was the site of several noteworthy Old Testament battles (Judges 5:19; 2 Kings 9:27; 23:29-30).

19. Campbell Robertson, "Iraq Suffers as the Euphrates River Dwindles," *New York Times*, July 13, 2009, www.nytimes.com/2009/07/14/world/middleeast/14euphrates.html?_r=0.

20. Revelation 16:13-14; superintending this action is the sovereign hand of God (Zechariah 14:2).

21. Joel 3:1-2; Zechariah 14:2-3.

22. With historical and theological hindsight, could there be any doubt that Satan was behind Hitler's efforts to rid

all Europe of Jews? Germany's dictator may have been the devil's attempt to bring Antichrist to reality in that era. But God decides the timing of prophetic fulfillment, not Satan.

23. Genesis 12:3; 27:29.

24. Romans 11:25-29.

25. Revelation 9:20-21; 16:9,11,21.

26. Daniel 7:13; Matthew 24:30; John 1:18; Revelation 1:7.

27. Revelation 6:2.

28. Acts 1:11.

29. Revelation 16:15.

30. Colossians 1:15; John 1:18; 14:9; Hebrews 1:3.

31. See also Revelation 2:16.

32. Luke 13:1-5.

33. Romans 5:10; 8:7; James 4:4; 1 John 2:15.

34. Revelation 19:12.

35. Revelation 2:17; 3:12.

36. Revelation 19:13; compare Isaiah 63:2-3.

37. Revelation 1:7, "and all the tribes of the earth will mourn over Him." *Mourn* in this context means to dread and fear the consequences of sin.

38. 2 Corinthians 6:2.

39. Genesis 7:16.

40. 2 Peter 3:1-9.

41. Revelation 19:7-8.

42. Revelation 17:14.

43. Revelation 7:13-14.

44. Matthew 25:31; 1 Thessalonians 1:7; Jude 14. Some also see Old Testament saints as part of this heavenly army (Zechariah 14:5).

45. Revelation 19:14.

46. John 1:43.

47. John 15:10-11.

48. Joshua 5:13-15.

49. Zechariah 14:4 (NIV).

50. The Mount of Olives is just east of Jerusalem across the Kidron Valley, and is where Jesus gathered His disciples to deliver stunning prophecies regarding the end times.

51. Jason Keyser, "Jerusalem's Old City at Risk in Earthquake," *NBC News*, January 19, 2004, www.nbcnews.com/id/3980139/ns/technology_and_sci ence-science/t/jerusalems-old-city-risk-earthquake/#.VJMqAcbbDRo.

52. Jeremiah 17:9; Romans 3:10-18,23; 6:23; 7:18.

53. Romans 8:29-30; 1 Corinthians 13:12; 15:49-51; 2 Corinthians 5:2-4.

54. Revelation 19:14. The use of the plural "armies" may suggest a certain order among the host that accompanies Christ, divided according to some category or rank.

55. Revelation 19:15.

56. Genesis 1:1; 2 Peter 3:5.

57. Hebrews 4:12.

58. 1 Timothy 4:6; Hebrews 5:11-14; 1 Peter 2:2.

59. Matthew 7:24-29; 16:15-18; Ephesians 5:25-26; 2 Timothy 3:16-17.

60. Ephesians 6:11-12,17.

61. 2 Peter 1:3-4.

62. Compare Revelation 19:15 with 14:18-20 and Isaiah 63:2-3.

63. Revelation 14:20. Whether this is meant to be taken literally, it pictures

the massive bloodbath that will occur when untold millions gather to fight Christ at Armageddon.

64. Revelation 19:15.

65. Hebrews 10:26-31.

66. Acts 17:30 (NIV).

67. Revelation 19:19. Revelation 16:13-16 also states that demons have gathered these armies together, signifying the satanic purpose of this great war.

Nevertheless it is God who superintends the overall scope of these events (Zechariah 14:2).

68. Revelation 19:16.

69. Revelation 19:21.

70. Matthew 24:28; Luke 17:37; Revelation 19:17-21. This is called "the great supper of God" (19:17).

71. Revelation 19:20.

Chapter 11: Heaven *Is* for Real, But You Haven't Been There…Yet

1. Bill Chappell, "Boy Says He Didn't Go to Heaven; Publisher Says It Will Pull Book," *The Two-Way*, January 15, 2015, www.npr.org/blogs/thetwo-way/2015/01/15/377589757/boy-says-he-didn-t-go-to-heaven-publisher-says-it-will-pull-book.

2. Todd Burpo, *Heaven Is for Real: A Little Boy's Astounding Story of His Trip to Heaven and Back* (Nashville, TN: Thomas Nelson, 2010).

3. 2 Corinthians 11:1-4.

4. Ephesians 4:14.

5. 2 Corinthians 13:5; Galatians 1:6-8.

6. Phil Johnson, "The Burpo-Malarkey Doctrine," *Grace to You* (blog), http://www.gty.org/Resources/Print/Blog/B121018.

7. 2 Corinthians 12:7.

8. Revelation 22:18-19.

9. 1 John 4:1; 2 Corinthians 13:5.

10. 2 Corinthians 11:13-15.

11. Ephesians 4:11-15. Though these stories may not technically constitute a "false gospel" as they relate to salvation, Paul nevertheless sternly warned

against receiving any other truth or teaching apart from God's revelation (Galatians 1:6-9).

12. 1 Timothy 4:1.

13. Isaiah 55:8-9.

14. 2 Corinthians 11:1-4.

15. Revelation 6–18; 19:17-21; 20:1-3.

16. Revelation 20:2-7. There are different interpretations concerning the millennial reign of Jesus. Godly men and scholars may disagree on the nature and timing of His reign, but on this one thing they all concur—Jesus is King and His kingdom lasts forever. For further study on the millennium, see Darrell Bock, *Three Views on the Millennium and Beyond* (Grand Rapids, MI: Zondervan, 1999).

17. Revelation 19:7-10; 22:5; Matthew 19:28; Luke 19:17-19; 1 Corinthians 6:3.

18. Why God allows this is not known. However it does prove, among other things, the inherent sinful nature of humanity. Believers alive during the Second Coming of Christ will go straight into the millennial kingdom.

But apparently children will be born during this time, and some among them will be deceived into following Satan in his last hurrah. Zechariah 14:16-19.

19. Revelation 20:7-10.

20. Revelation 20:11-15. The lake of fire refers to God's eternal, unrelenting wrath upon all those who refuse salvation in Christ. Whatever kind of fire this represents, it will be much worse than that on earth.

21. Mark 3:14.

22. John 14:3.

23. John 17:24.

24. Revelation 21:3.

25. Philippians 1:21-25.

26. Revelation 21:1; Isaiah 65:17; Matthew 24:35; 2 Peter 3:7,10-13.

27. Galatians 4:26; Hebrews 11:10; 12:22-24; 13:14.

28. Revelation 21:9.

29. Revelation 21:6-7.

30. *Expositors Bible Commentary*, vol. 12, ed. Frank E. Gaebelein (Grand Rapids, MI: Zondervan, 1981), 593.

31. Isaiah 65:20.

32. Revelation 14:11.

33. Romans 8:18.

34. Ecclesiastes 2:25; James 1:17. God is the author of all true fun and enjoyment.

35. Revelation 21:5.

36. C.S. Lewis. *Letters to Malcom: Chiefly on Prayer* (Orlando: Harcourt, 1964), 93.

37. 1 Corinthians 15:20,23,42-44; Colossians 1:18; 1 John 3:2-3; Revelation 1:5.

38. Romans 8:30; 1 Corinthians 15:51-53.

39. 1 Corinthians 15:42-43.

40. 1 Timothy 6:16.

41. John 20:19.

42. Luke 24:31; John 20:19,26; Acts 1:9-11.

43. Matthew 8:11; Luke 22:18; 24:39-43; Revelation 19:9.

44. Mark Hitchcock, *The End* (Carol Stream, IL: Tyndale House, 2012), 453.

45. Hebrews 11:10.

46. All these descriptions come from Revelation 21:10–22:5.

47. Hitchcock, *The End*, 454.

48. Revelation 22:3.

49. Matthew 8:11; 1 Thessalonians 4:17.

50. Revelation 14:13.

51. Matthew 17:1-14; 8:11.

52. Matthew 22:24-30; 1 Corinthians 7:31.

53. See Ephesians 1:4, 13-14; 2 Corinthians 11:2-3; John 14:1-3, Revelation 19:7.

54. Revelation 19:9.

55. Matthew 8:11; 22:1-4; 25:1-13; Luke 14:16-24.

56. Revelation 21:8,27.

57. Revelation 5:12.

58. Revelation 22:1-5.

Chapter 12: The Beauty Awakes

1. www.pitt.edu/~dash/type0410.html.

2. Revelation was meant to enlighten and awaken the church worldwide in John's day, as it is meant to do in ours. I believe the seven churches are representative of churches then and now (e.g., Galatians, Corinthians).

3. 2 Timothy 3:16-17.

4. Acts 20:27.

5. 2 Timothy 4:1-5.

6. Ephesians 6:17.

7. 1 Timothy 4:6.

8. Ephesians 4:11-16.

9. Luke 10:38-42.

10. Luke 14:34-35.

11. John 3:30.

12. John 1:19-27.

13. Matthew 11:11.

14. John 3:29; Matthew 11:11.

15. Romans 12:3.

16. Revelation 2:10-11; 3:12.

17. Revelation 3:19.

18. Ephesians 5:25-27; 1 Samuel 15:22.

19. Ephesians 5:23-24.

20. Matthew 10:37-39; 22:37-39.

21. John 14:15.

22. John 13:34-35.

23. John 15:10.

24. Revelation 2:5.

25. 1 Corinthians 3:15.

26. Revelation 2:5; 3:3.

27. 1 Corinthians 11:24-26.

28. 1 John 1:8–2:3.

29. Revelation 3:19.

30. Ecclesiastes 5:1-7.

31. Luke 17:3; Romans 8:29; 2 Corinthians 7:9.

32. Revelation 2:5.

33. See Acts 19–20.

34. 1 Thessalonians 1:10.

35. Titus 2:13.

36. Romans 13:11-12.

37. 1 Thessalonians 5:6.

38. 1 Peter 1:13.

39. 1 Peter 1:14-16; 1 John 3:3.

40. 1 Thessalonians 5:23; 1 John 2:28.

41. 1 Thessalonians 4:18; 1 Peter 1:3.

42. Psalm 90:1-2,12; Ephesians 5:5-17.

43. Job 7:7; Psalm 39:4-6; Proverbs 27:1; James 4:13-17.

44. Matthew 25:14-30.

45. Matthew 20:1-16.

46. Revelation 3:20.

47. Matthew 10:37-39; 22:36-37.

48. He reiterates this in Revelation 22:16.

49. Revelation 2:7,11,17,29; 3:6,13,22.

50. Revelation 22:6.

51. Revelation 22:10,12.

52. Revelation 22:17.

53. Revelation 22:20.

About the Author

Jeff Kinley (ThM, Dallas Theological Seminary) empowers people with vintage truth. Jeff is the author of over 20 books, including *As It Was in the Days of Noah,* and speaks all over the country. He and his wife live in Arkansas and have three grown sons.

**See jeffkinley.com for more information
about his ministry.**

Also by Jeff Kinley

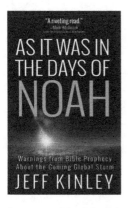

The story of Noah is one of the most captivating in all the Bible. Yet most people remember it mainly as a children's story found in picture books and heard in Sunday school classes.

But this tragedy really took place—and widely overlooked is Jesus's stunning prophecy that the final days of planet Earth would be just as it was in the days of Noah. His point? That there would be striking parallels between Noah's day and the end times—with warnings of God's imminent judgment upon the world.

Is Jesus's prophecy now being fulfilled? And if yes, how then should we respond?

As It Was in the Days of Noah explores the similarities between the two periods, such as the rapid rise in evil and increasingly flagrant disregard for God. A powerful resource that...

- examines the signs that we're nearing the end times
- affirms the urgency of reaching the lost with God's compassion and truth
- equips you to live wisely and "redeem the time" so it counts for eternity

The Fifth Gospel
Bobby Conway with Jeff Kinley

"There are five Gospels:
Matthew, Mark, Luke, John...and the Christian.
But most people never read the first four."

There are any number of books on how to *do* evangelism. This book is different—it's an invitation to actually *live out* the message of the gospel. Jesus's original intention was for ordinary people like you and me to live lives that point others to the only Person who can give them hope for this life as well as the next—to visibly display the Good News of salvation through the Messiah and Redeemer of humankind.

But many Christ followers today are either ridden with guilt for not telling others about Jesus or so silent that no one really knows they're a Christian. *The Fifth Gospel* will help you wrestle with the critical issues involved in living out your faith in front of a watching and sometimes not-so-friendly world.

Isn't it time to become a witness for the One you profess to love? Prepare yourself to represent your Savior well and to discover a new way to do evangelism. Get ready for God to unleash the gospel through you!

To learn more about Harvest House books and
to read sample chapters, visit our website:

www.harvesthousepublishers.com

HARVEST HOUSE PUBLISHERS
EUGENE, OREGON